Shaping Your Child's Sexual Identity

Shaping Your Child's Sexual Identity

George Alan Rekers

BAKER BOOK HOUSE
Grand Rapids, Michigan 49506

Books by Dr. Rekers:
The Christian in an Age of Sexual Eclipse
(with Michael Braun)

Growing Up Straight: What Families Need to Know about Homosexuality

Shaping Your Child's Sexual Identity

ISBN: 0-8010-7713-3

Library of Congress Catalog Card Number: 82-70461

Printed in the United States of America

Scripture references are from the New International Version of the Bible, copyright 1978 by New York International Bible Society.

To my three sons,
Steve, Andy,** and **Matt,
with affection.

While most of my professional work has been dedicated to helping other parents help their children, I hope that I'll always be available first and foremost as a helpful father to my own boys.

In my practice of child psychology I've benefited from being a father myself. What the textbooks and formal training couldn't teach me about childrearing, my own children have taught me and continue to teach me. So it is only fitting that I lovingly acknowledge these three very special ones who have brought so much joy to Sharon and me.

Contents

Foreword

We live in an age of increasing confusion and debate regarding family roles. In the past twenty years in particular, America has experienced a considerable deterioration of commitment to the responsible roles of fathers and mothers, husbands and wives. The Office for Families monitors the symptoms of this trend as we collect statistics showing a disturbing rise in the rates of marital separation, divorce, adolescent pregnancy, and runaway youth. I hope to see these trends reversed by a new understanding of and commitment to clear male and female roles in American family life.

Our country needs a widespread return to the genuine masculine role of being a dedicated father and a faithful husband. The images of the macho male and the male chauvinist need to be seen as counterfeit masculinity. Insensitive assertion and promiscuous conquest are spurious stereotypes of masculinity. A true male identity is reflected in the caring and protective role of the responsible father and husband.

As men live responsible masculine roles, much of the hurt and conflict behind the current controversy over women's roles will subside. Certainly there is equality in the worth and dignity of both women and men, but this does not imply that there is no distinction between male and female identity.

In this book, Dr. Rekers draws the clear distinction between harmful sex-role stereotypes on the one hand and the essence of true masculinity and femininity on the other hand. He exposes the dangers of the naïve unisex mentality for family life; but most significantly, he charts the way that will allow parents to lead boys and girls to have healthy sexual identities. Dr. Rekers's prescriptions are based on child-development research and the historic truths of the Judeo-Christian ethic.

When these prescriptions are followed by men and women, boys and girls, we will see a major restoration of family life in our own time. To this end I commend this book to you and your family.

> Jerry Regier
> Associate Commissioner
> Administration for Children,
>   Youth and Families
> Director, Office for Families
> U.S. Department of Health and Human Services

> May 1, 1982

Acknowledgments

I have largely devoted the past ten years of my career as a psychologist to research and counseling designed to help parents shape normal sexual identities in their children. This means that I cannot possibly hope to be able to acknowledge all the people who enabled me to gain expertise on this topic. Nevertheless, I will express my gratitude to a few individuals who represent a large number of others for whom I am also thankful.

I was privileged to have Dr. O. Ivar Lovaas, a world-renowned child psychologist, as my major professor when I studied for my Ph.D. degree in psychology at the University of California, Los Angeles. He assigned me a clinical research project on childhood sexual-identity problems which eventually became the basis for my dissertation. My doctoral study at UCLA was supported by a graduate fellowship from the National Science Foundation, which I gratefully acknowledge.

When I was appointed a visiting scholar at the Center for the Behavioral Sciences at Harvard University, I had a grant from the Foundations' Fund for Research in Psychiatry to further extend my study in this area of sexual-identity development. As a university professor and as the president of the Logos Research Institute, Inc., I received major clinical research grants totaling more than half a million dollars from the National Institute of Mental Health to conduct research on sexual-identity disorders in children (United States Public Health Service Research Grants MH21803, MH28240, and MH29945, the last at the Logos Research Institute, Inc.). Not only do I gratefully acknowledge these sources of research funding, but I also express appreciation for the collaboration and consultation of many colleagues, including Peter M. Bentler, Alexander C. Rosen, Judson J. Swihart, Judy Sanders, Barbara F. Crandall, Gilbert C. Milner III, Larry N. Ferguson, Michael Mecherikoff, Shasta L. Mead, and Stephen Brigham. I also express warm thanks to Ed Welge, former chairman of the board of directors, Bill Rehwald, former member of the board of directors, and Judd Swihart, vice president and board member of the Logos Research Institute, Inc., which has sponsored my research for many years in supportive ways that are too numerous to mention. In a real sense, they made my long-term research project possible.

More than anyone else, my friend, Reed Bell, Chief of Pediatrics at Sacred Heart Hospital in Pensacola, Florida, inspired me and then encouraged me over several years to see this book to its final completion. His vision for a book like this for parents sparked my original interest in this writing project.

Sometimes I think that I have learned more about parenting from my own experience as a foster parent to four boys and girls, aged four to sixteen, and from my role as a father of my own three sons, Steven, Andrew, and Matthew, than I have from my professional experiences. Of course, my wife, Sharon, has been my lifelong partner in this exciting challenge of family life. I was able to write this book only with my family's loving cooperation.

Part ONE

Casualties in Families

As a clinical child psychologist, I am often asked these kinds of questions by concerned mothers and fathers:

Should boys and girls be reared differently?

Aren't male and female roles changing so rapidly that it makes sense to rear children in a unisex role?

When is the tomboy phase normal and when is it abnormal?

Should I be concerned if my boy is called a sissy and prefers feminine play activities?

Should the mother and father have equal roles in the family, or should the father be the family leader?

The three chapters in this section introduce these topics and clarify the issues involved in families where the children are developing confused sexual identities. Many boys and girls are casualties of families where proper sex-role training is lacking. Every parent can learn more about shaping a child's sexual identity by carefully considering what went wrong in the families I am about to describe. If we parents can learn from the mistakes of others, we will not risk the well-being of our own children.

1

1

The Unisex Myth

A fierce battle is being waged today over male and female roles in family life. For thousands of years of Western culture, the overwhelming majority of people accepted and lived according to some basic distinctions between the roles of mothers and fathers, wives and husbands. The only legitimate way for a child to be born and reared was in a heterosexual marriage, providing both a mother and father to jointly share in the rights and responsibilities of family life. Unmarried motherhood was considered tragic for the child because of the absence of a supportive father who should have a role in cooperatively insuring a protective family environment for the child. Boys were reared somewhat differently than girls were. Boys were dressed somewhat differently than girls were. Boys were encouraged to identify with their fathers and other men, and girls were encouraged to identify with their mothers and other women. A person's sex was considered to be an important distinction in human personality. But now this idea that sex makes a difference is being fought against by vocal and active social reformers.

One of the official goals of the National Organization for Women (NOW) is to work toward "an end to all distinctions based on sex."[1] This is a concise definition of the unisex mentality which is gaining popularity in our society today. When advocates of unisex childrearing publish their ideas, it becomes immediately clear that when they argue for "an end to *all* distinctions based on sex" (italics mine), they

1. Mary Samith et al., *Revolution: Tomorrow is NOW* (National Organization for Women, 1973), p. 9. This publication is described on page 1 as "a summary of NOW's existing resolutions and policies by issue."

3

include distinctions between men and women as sexual partners. In other words, they say that a woman should be free to choose either a man or a woman for a sexual partner, and that an openly practicing lesbian is as fit to be a mother as is a heterosexual, married woman.[2]

Should the family be based upon a heterosexual marriage? Should the mother's role in the family be different, in some significant respects, from the father's role? Does the child's long-term sexual identity and normal sexual adjustment depend, in some way, upon a unique fathering from the father and a unique mothering from the mother? The unisex advocates say no to all of these questions.

A "Myth of Motherhood"?

With increasing volume and frequency, feminists are taking critical aim at what they call the "myth of motherhood."[3] In fact, the radical feminists are opposed to the traditional heterosexual marriage as the basis for family life and childrearing:

> The end of the institution of marriage is a necessary condition for the liberation of women. Therefore, it is important for us to encourage women to leave their husbands and not live individually with men. We must build alternatives to marriage.[4]

2. *Ibid.*, pp. 20 – 21. See also page 27 of the *National Plan of Action* (Washington, DC: International Women's Year Commission, 1977), adopted at the National Women's Conference, November 18 – 21, 1977, in Houston, Texas. This publication states, "This National Plan of Action constitutes the official recommendations of the National Women's Conference, pursuant to Public Law 94 – 167."

3. Rachel T. Hare-Mustin and Patricia C. Broderick, "The Motherhood Inventory: A Questionnaire for Studying Attitudes toward Motherhood" (paper presented at the annual meeting of the American Psychological Association, Toronto, August 1978); Rachel T. Hare-Mustin, "A Feminist Approach to Family Therapy," *Family Process* 17 (1978): 181 – 194; Angela B. McBride, *The Growth and Development of Mothers* (New York: Harper and Row, 1973); B. Rollin, "Motherhood: Who Needs It?" *Look*, September 22, 1970; Samuel L. Blumenfeld, *The Retreat from Motherhood* (New Rochelle, NY: Arlington House, 1975); B. E. Lott, " 'Who Wants Children?' . . . Some Relationships among Attitudes towards Children, Parents, and the Liberation of Women," *American Psychologist* 28 (1973): 573 – 582. For a further discussion of motherhood in twentieth-century America, see Michael Braun and George Alan Rekers, *The Christian in an Age of Sexual Eclipse* (Wheaton, IL: Tyndale, 1981), chapter 7, "Out of the Shadows: The Woman's Role."

4. Nancy Lehmann and Helen Sullinger, *The Document: Declaration of Feminism* (Minneapolis: Powderhorn Station, 1972), pp. 11 – 12.

The feminists' unisex notion of childrearing assumes that there should be no difference between the mother's and father's roles, and that children need not even be reared in a nuclear family with both a male and a female parent. According to the radical feminists, children would be better reared in federally-funded, "nonsexist" child-care centers:[5]

> The nuclear family must be replaced with a new form of family where individuals live and work together to help meet the needs of all people in the society.[6]

> We support parent-controlled child care centers as a necessary step toward the feminist-socialist revolution, but our vision of the upbringing of children extends beyond them. With the destruction of the nuclear family must come a new way of looking at children. They must be seen as the responsibility of an *entire society* rather than individual parents. . . .[7]

NOW has made similar pleas for the overthrow of the ideal of a heterosexual marriage as the context for care for children.[8] In fact, feminist rhetoric often goes so far as to suggest that "parents are unnecessary" for childrearing and that children might be better reared by various child-care workers and teachers.[9] And the unisex notion further dictates that the child's books and child-care experiences should be nonsexist, that is, ". . . to remove all references to 'ideal' or 'normal,' 'masculine' or 'feminine' etiquette, social behavior and vocations. . . ."[10]

One of the resolutions of NOW states:

5. *National Plan of Action*, p. 7. This proposal states, in part, "The Federal government should assume a major role in directing and providing comprehensive, voluntary, flexible-hour, bias-free, non-sexist, quality child care and developmental programs, including child care facilities for Federal employees and should request and support adequate legislation and funding for these programs."

6. Lehmann and Sullinger, *The Document: Declaration of Feminism*, p. 13.

7. *Ibid.*, p. 14.

8. Samith et al., *Revolution: Tomorrow Is NOW*.

9. *National Plan of Action*. For an extended discussion of the radical feminist approach to children, parenting, and family life, see Braun and Rekers, *The Christian in an Age of Sexual Eclipse*, chapter 3, "Drawing the Battle Line: The Radical Challenge of Sexual Extremists."

10. Samith et al., *Revolution: Tomorrow Is NOW*, p. 9.

Realizing that each individual child has the capacity for the full range of human characteristics, the child should not be channeled into a role based on sexual stereotypes. Further research must be undertaken to discover ways to prevent sex-role channeling.[11]

In other words, the proponents of unisex childrearing want to obliterate the meaning of masculinity and femininity. They don't want children to be exposed to male roles from fathers and female roles from mothers. They do not want children to be taught that there is a difference between male and female roles. In short, they advocate training both boys and girls in a unisex role. Ironically, these ardent unisexists deplore the preoccupation of little girls with baby dolls and frilly dresses, but they strongly defend and endorse the right of little boys to play with dolls and dresses.[12]

The Source of Unisex Notions

The unisex notions are not based upon the findings of child-development research. (I will review such research in chapter 3.) Instead, the feminist and unisex ideas are rooted in the relativism of humanistic thinking.[13] These ideas are based on the world view which rejects the philosophical idea of antithesis.[14] The idea of natural sex-role boundaries embedded in creation is anathema to the

11. *Ibid.*, p. 15.

12. Richard Green, "Sexual Differentiation in the Human Male and Female: Science, Strategies, and Politics," in *Progress in Sexology*, ed. Robert Gemme and Connie Christine Wheeler (New York and London: Plenum, 1977), p. 8.

13. See the extended discussion of the relationship between secular humanism and feminist thinking in Braun and Rekers, *The Christian in an Age of Sexual Eclipse*, chapter 2, "The Rhetoric of Revolt: The Sexual Propaganda of Humanism."

14. The word *antithesis* has been defined this way: "Direct opposition or contrast between two things. (As in 'joy' which is the *antithesis* of 'sorrow.')" This definition is offered by philosopher Francis A. Shaeffer in *The God Who Is There* (Downers Grove, IL: Inter-Varsity, 1968). Shaeffer points out, ". . . much modern homosexuality is an expression of the current denial of antithesis. It has led in this case to an obliteration of the distinction between man and woman. So the male and the female as complementary partners are finished. This is a foremost homosexuality which is a part of the movement below the line of despair. But this is not an isolated problem; it is a part of the world-spirit of the generation which surrounds us. It is imperative that Christians realise the conclusions which are being drawn as a result of the death of absolute" (p. 39).

relativistic humanists.[15] Traditionally, the concept of antithesis would clarify that choosing a male sexual mate is a feminine sex-role behavior, properly the role of the female. However, the relativistic humanists do not hold up heterosexuality as a desired norm:

> . . . neither do we wish to prohibit, by law or social sanction, sexual behavior between consenting adults. The many varieties of sexual exploration should not in themselves be considered "evil." Short of harming others or compelling them to do likewise, individuals should be permitted to express their sexual proclivities and pursue their lifestyles as they desire.[16]

So the proponents of unisex childrearing do not believe that children should be taught that committing oneself to marital fidelity to a woman for a lifetime is a masculine thing for a man to do. The unisexist would be just as happy if a man had sexual relations with another man. After all, the word *unisex* means that a person's sex doesn't make any difference! This is not a conclusion reached on the basis of scientific research. It is simply the idea of a relativistic, humanistic world view.

The unisex myth is being widely propagated in the media in the latter quarter of the twentieth century. But what is the effect of this myth upon individual lives and upon our social order?

Let's consider an actual case to bring this notion into a practical, real-life perspective. Details of this case have been altered to conceal the girl's identity.

A Distraught Daughter

Julie is a fourteen-year-old girl whose pediatrician referred her to me for psychological help. I met her in the waiting room and walked

---

15. See *Humanist Manifestos One and Two* (Buffalo, NY: Prometheus Books, 1973). For example, *Humanist Manifesto Two* states, "We affirm that moral values derive their source from human experience. Ethics are autonomous and situational, needing no theological or ideological sanction. Ethics stem from human need and interest. . . . We strive for the good life, here and now" (p. 17); "We believe in maximum individual autonomy consonant with social responsibility. Although science can account for the causes of behavior, the possibilities of individual freedom of choice exist in human life and should be increased" (p. 18). See also David W. Ehrenfeld, *The Arrogance of Humanism* (New York: Oxford University Press, 1978).

16. *Humanist Manifesto Two*, p. 18.

with her down the corridor to my office. She was wearing a black leather jacket, a boy's shirt, blue jeans, and tennis shoes.

For the first few minutes of the interview, I had Julie describe her family to me. Her mother had been divorced twice and the family had moved fifteen times in the past six years. Since her preschool years, Julie had not had a stable father figure in the home, although her mother had had many boyfriends. She had a seventeen-year-old sister and a seven-year-old sister.

I asked Julie, "So there's the three of you girls? Do you all have the same father?"

"I don't know," she replied.

There were many such details that Julie could not recall regarding her family life. Because the family had moved so many times, she was not certain of any of the dates of the moves from state to state.

Feeling Feminine?

After we had developed some rapport in our conversation, I told Julie that her pediatrician had let me know that she had confided in him that she would rather be a man than a woman. I asked her, "Well, why don't you tell a little bit about your feelings about what it's like to be a girl, and your feelings that you might not want to be a girl?"

Julie said, "Well, I've—I've always felt like a guy. . . . I've never felt like a girl. Not that I can remember."

"Mm-hum."

Julie added, "I just knew. See, one thing about me is that I am shy and nobody really pays that much attention. But you know, just last year I told my guidance counselor."

"I see, you felt comfortable with telling your guidance counselor."

"Yeah, we talked. But you know, the first one I ever told was my best friend. Her name is Sally, she understands my problem."

"So Sally understands you well. How long ago did you tell her?"

"Well, I told her, I believe, when I was in the sixth grade. You know. Just last year, I think."

"I see."

"Now, I told . . . see I only tell my close friends that know me that well. The ones I trust. You know?"

"You feel comfortable telling just the friends that you trust, is that what you mean?"

"It's kind of difficult explaining it to the guidance counselor, you know what I mean?"

"Yes, that would be hard."

"Oh, yeah."

"Was that a woman or a man guidance counselor?"

"Woman."

"Um-hum. So actually you have told a couple of your trusted friends first. Then later on, the next person you told was your guidance counselor."

"Yeah."

"And then this year you told your pediatrician, Dr. Doe."

"Yes. He understood pretty well, and he thought I needed some help."

"And then did Dr. Doe tell your mom?"

"Yeah."

"And since that time have you and your mom talked about it?"

"No."

By Any Other Name?

Julie explained that she had "felt like a guy" for as long as she could remember. She could not recall any interest in the games or feminine activities that are typical of girls in their early and late childhood.

Julie also preferred to be called "John" instead of "Julie," but many of her friends gave her the nickname "Mick" or "Mickey," which closely reflected one of her favorite rock stars. Her mother told me that "John" and "Mick" are the names of her rock-star idols and that she has their pictures and posters on the wall in her bedroom.

Is Life Worth Living?

Julie frequently suffered depression so severe that she would contemplate suicide. She had mentally prepared all the details of a suicide plan, and intended to use a gun that she knew her mother had at home. She had not yet made a suicide attempt, but in one instance she had threatened suicide and her teacher at school had talked her out of taking her own life.

I asked Julie, "So you have felt so frustrated that you have even thought through how you could kill yourself. Does your mom know that you ever felt that way?"

Julie replied, "No."

I determined from further interviewing and psychological testing that Julie was not currently contemplating suicide, and that she should be involved in psychological treatment in order to avoid the risk that she might attempt suicide.

A Hope Chest? A Proposal?

I also asked Julie, "When you have thought of growing up, have you considered the possibility that you may want to get married some day?"

"No. I've always thought I would be single."

"And now at fourteen years old, you've probably begun to mature physically as a woman, right?"

Julie, mumbling with disgust, said, "Um-hum."

"Does that bother you?"

"Sometimes."

"Because that's not what you want?"

"Yeah. Yesterday on TV I saw, you know, that tennis player that was a guy but had an operation and is a girl now."

"Yes, there are some people who have had operations to change their sexual appearance."

"She's on TV. Her name is Renee Richards. I think he used to be called Richard somebody, but now her name is Renee Richards."

"Some people have thought that if they could only change their bodies to match their minds, that they would be happier. But other people, especially teen-agers, have been able to work on a different kind of answer. They might say, 'My body is a girl so if I can only change my mind to want to be a girl, then I'd be happier.'"

"I've always thought that I'd rather change my body to be more like my mind. I heard that there was somebody named Judy on TV who had an operation and changed her name to Jude."

"Actually, you should know that doctors do not perform that kind of operation as much any more and that, in any event, they cannot legally do it for a teen-ager."

"Well, I've just got to have an operation. Because, you know, I'm always checking out the girls. You know what I mean? I fall in love with girls and not with boys. And I don't want to be a queer. So I've got to have an operation to change my body into a man so that I could make love with my girl friends."

Faltering Femininity

Julie's case was a complicated one. I conducted an extensive psychological evaluation which included clinical psychological testing. Julie also had an evaluation by a pediatric endocrinologist, who found her to be physically normal in every way.

Julie's mother told me that Julie's desire to be a boy became evident to her only during the past year. Julie, on the other hand, insisted that she had always felt like a boy. Similarly, Julie's mother described her as being "the same as other girls" until the past year, but Julie denied ever being interested in typically feminine play activities during her early or late childhood. Julie's mother's impression was that her daughter was simply going through a tomboy stage and for this reason her mother was not concerned about Julie's attitude. Her mother said that Julie's older sister, Mary, went through a "similar phase" and for this reason she expected that Julie would grow out of her masculine identification, just as her older sister had.

"One of the Boys"?

Most of Julie's friends were girls. This fact, taken alone, is typical of other girls her age. But Julie's interest in girls was quite different than normal. When she described her girl friends, her attitude toward them was primarily one of sexual interest. She spoke of how pretty they were and how well-built they were—much as a teen-age boy might do.

At school, Julie usually ate lunch with a group of boys, and she said "we" when she referred to this group. For some time, she had taken F's in her gym class because her coach would not allow her to play on the boys' team. She refused to play with the girls' teams and sat on the bench instead during gym class. She reacted negatively to her physical maturation, refusing to wear a bra and always neglecting to tell her mother when she needed feminine hygiene articles.

Unisex or Cross-sex?

On each visit to the clinic, Julie dressed in a stereotypically masculine manner. She never wore a dress or a skirt. She always wore blue jeans or corduroy jeans along with men's T-shirts or men's shirts. She wore tennis shoes or boots. Her gestures and mannerisms were hypermasculine, that is, an exaggeration of masculine gestures. When she spoke, she projected her voice into the lowest possible register to imitate a masculine voice.

I found that Julie had a dull normal intelligence. Her psychological test scores indicated that she was inclined toward masculine interests and activities. Her keenest interests were in hunting, camping, riding motorcycles, riding horses, playing football and baseball, and building race-car models. On the various psychological test forms, she indicated that she always wished to be a boy, that she never enjoyed romantic love stories, that she had never dated a boy, and that she had never been romantically interested in boys.

In terms of her overall personality, Julie's testing profile indicated that she was introverted, unpredictable, and sometimes peculiar in action and thought. Individuals who score as she did on her testing usually experience subtle communication problems with other people. They have impaired empathy and find it difficult to become emotionally involved with others. Such people frequently act in self-defeating ways and have difficulty evaluating social situations. While they are often angry with others, they are unable to handle or express such feelings in appropriate ways. They therefore have the potential for antisocial behavior.

Questions for Parents

Julie's mother was tragically unaware of the distress signals that Julie had given for many years. In fact, Julie's mother was comforted by all she heard on television and radio about changing sex roles and the new trend toward eliminating all sex-role stereotypes. With the "greater tolerance" by society, she felt certain that Julie would do just fine if she continued in her masculine preferences. "After all," Julie's mother thought, "the distinction between masculine and feminine is fading away anyway."

This was a mother who didn't know the difference between a normal tomboy phase and the early symptoms of sexual-identity disturbance in her daughter. But this is not unusual. Most parents have not been trained to detect the early signs of sexual-identity disturbance. This book was written to help concerned parents learn to recognize these early warning signs.

Secret Struggles

Finally, I should note that Julie, like so many teen-agers, had not told her mother the complete story about her sexual-identity struggles. This makes it all the more important for parents to be alert to the signs and symptoms of sexual-identity problems, in order to be of help.

Early Warnings

Now that I have reviewed Julie's case, a concerned parent might ask, "What is the way of detecting these kinds of problems at an early age in order to prevent the misery associated with sexual-identity confusion in the teen-age years?"

The answer to this question is not a simple one, and it will take this entire book to provide the basis for that answer.

We will see that there are certain behavior patterns in childhood which are associated with a very high risk for the development of a tendency toward a sexual abnormality in later life. For example, in most cases, men involved in homosexuality have reported specific feminine behavior patterns indicative of a difficulty in adjusting to the male role in early childhood.[17] Similarly, while a tomboy phase is normal in 60 percent of all girls, we will see in chapter 7 that there is a pattern of masculine identification and masculine role adoption by girls in childhood which can be distinguished from tomboyism and which places the girl at high risk for homosexual temptation in the teen-age years and adulthood.[18] But this is a complex distinction between the normal tomboy phase and sexual-identity confusion. The unisex mentality is much too simplistic to help parents tell the difference.

Unisex Myth

Did the unisex notion help or confuse Julie and her mother? What continuing damage will the unisex notion create for Julie and other

17. F. L. Whitam, "Childhood indicators of male homosexuality," *Archives of Sexual Behavior* 6 (1977): 89 – 96; B. Zuger, "Effeminate behavior present in boys from childhood: Ten additional years of follow-up," *Comprehensive Psychiatry* 19 (1978): 363 – 369; G. A. Rekers et al., "Child gender disturbances: A clinical rationale for intervention," *Psychotherapy: Theory, Research, and Practice* 14 (1977): 2 – 11.

18. G. A. Rekers and S. L. Mead, "Female sex-role deviance: Early identification and developmental intervention," *Journal of Clinical Child Psychology* 9, no. 3 (1980): 199 – 203.

youth in the future? What impact did the feminist viewpoint have on Julie? Will this viewpoint help her solve her depression and sexual-identity confusion?

From a psychological viewpoint, Julie was suffering from sexual-identity confusion which resulted from growing up in a family where there was incorrect and incomplete training given to her about proper male and female roles. Her sexual-identity problem was a result, in part, of her abnormal relationships with father figures. Her mother failed to provide her with proper training and encouragement in the female role. Consequently, Julie did not accept her femininity, and she rejected her female identity.

The feminists preach "an end to all distinctions based on sex," but there *is* a distinction between male and female, and Julie had failed to learn that distinction. Because Julie failed to learn about and accept her uniqueness as a female, she was both psychologically and socially maladjusted. Julie wanted a female lover who would accept her in a masculine role, but all the girls to whom she was sexually attracted were uninterested in her and had plans of eventually marrying a man. So Julie was a misfit.

Once we recognize the absurdity of the unisex myth and the feminist myth, we are faced with the question, "Why do so many people accept these myths?" At the same time, we wonder, "If clear distinctions between male and female roles are necessary in rearing boys and girls to avoid Julie's kind of problem, why do so many parents today experiment with the dangerous unisex ideas in their families?"

The Male Chauvinist Mentality

For many people, the unisex mentality is a simple-minded over-reaction to the equally menacing macho male chauvinist mentality. C. S. Lewis was right when he observed that errors in the world come in pairs—opposite pairs. People see one evil and run blindly away from it into the arms of its opposite extreme. Decades ago, people were likely to be blind to the evils of male chauvinism, but today the pernicious effects of male chauvinism are commonly recognized. Staring at the clear and present dangers of male chauvinism, modern people back into the blind alley of unisex nonsense without clearly noticing its equally destructive consequences.

The Macho Menace

Both history and contemporary experience provide too many examples of men who have maintained the grossly discriminatory attitude that women are generally inferior to men in any important aspect of personality or capability. Instead of letting each individual demonstrate his ability, the male chauvinist has arrogantly, unlovingly, and unfairly ruled women out of many social opportunities on the basis of their sex. History records that thousands upon thousands of women have been denied education, the right to vote, and the right to own property, for example, purely on the basis of presumed male superiority in these matters.[19]

The macho mentality defines masculinity in terms of sexual conquest of woman after woman, which becomes the basis for bragging. Masculinity to a macho male may be repairing a Mack truck, having a tattoo, or insensitively plowing through the corporate jungle. The macho male does not cry or express tender emotions of caring—he can "gut it out," with pride in his self-sufficient strength.

True Masculinity

But this macho image is a destructive distortion of true masculinity. It is *not* true masculinity. Macho is promiscuous; true masculinity commits itself to a permanent and faithful bond to a woman in marriage. Macho exploits women for its own advantage; true masculinity treats women with respect, caring, and assistance. Macho expresses no tender emotion; true masculinity can cry, love, and care.[20] "Greater love has no one than this, that one lay down his life for his friends" (John 15:13).

No wonder many women have banded together to oppose male chauvinism and the macho mentality. Historically, a women's movement was necessary to win the vote and other important social rights

19. Every generation seems to have some category of human beings who are singled out for gross discrimination by denying them their human rights in order to suit the convenience of another group of people. In some ages, males have pursued their own advantage by denying human rights to females. In other times, whites have pursued their own advantage by denying human rights to blacks. In our own time, adults are pursuing their own advantage by denying human rights (i.e., the right to life) to their unborn children. See Francis A. Shaeffer and C. Everett Koop, *Whatever Happened to the Human Race?* (Old Tappan, NJ: Revell, 1979). See also Francis A. Shaeffer et al., *Plan for Action* (Old Tappan, NJ: Revell, 1980).

20. See Braun and Rekers, *The Christian in an Age of Sexual Eclipse*, chapter 8, "Reflecting God's Glory: The Man's Role."

for women. But the radical feminists of today have focused so single-mindedly upon the evils of male chauvinism that they have swung to the opposite extreme of endorsing the evils of a unisex mentality.[21]

In their attempt to discard the harmful and arbitrary male and female stereotypes generated by male chauvinism, feminists have mistakenly called for "an end to all distinctions based on sex." The good is thrown out with the bad, and the result is just as wrong as the evil they were trying to overcome.

Are *all* male and female roles invalid? Should *all* sex-role differences be abolished? Of course not. We need to be careful to sort out the wheat from the tares. We can deliberately teach our children about the evils of male chauvinism without throwing away the concept of sex roles altogether!

If sex roles have been abused, we should not throw away the concept of distinct sexual identities as though it doesn't matter. Because drugs are sometimes abused, we do not outlaw the proper use of medicine. Instead, we teach our children the difference between the proper use of drugs and the misuse of them. In the same way, we need to teach our children the proper male and female roles and to school them against the excesses of male chauvinism and the menacing macho myth.

A Different Standard

NOW has a membership of less than .1 percent of the United States population. And yet its unisex and feminist values are loudly proclaimed in the mass media.

In sharp contrast, national polls[22] report that 90 percent of all Americans "favor the Christian religion." Ninety percent of Americans pray to God. Eighty percent insist that they believe Jesus to be God or the Son of God. Seventy percent of all Americans are church members. (This is a marked increase from less than 10 percent of all Americans being church members during the Revolutionary War, and

21. See Braun and Rekers, *The Christian in an Age of Sexual Eclipse*, chapter 3, "Drawing the Battle Lines: The Radical Challenge of Sexual Extremists."

22. 1978 Harris Poll and 1979 Gallup Poll. These same statistics were reported by Kenneth Kantzer, editor of *Christianity Today*, in a commencement speech to the graduating class of Trinity Evangelical Divinity School, Arnold T. Olson Chapel, May 1979, Deerfield, Illinois.

no more than 20 percent being church members throughout nineteenth-century America.)

More than 50 percent of all Americans claim to have had a born-again conversion experience to Christ, and at least 40 percent claim they are evangelical. Thirty-three percent of Americans confess Jesus Christ as their "only hope of heaven," and 25 percent of the population insist that the Bible is inerrant.

If I quote from the *Humanist Manifesto* and the radical feminists who constitute a tiny fraction of the population in America, I would hardly be out of place to quote the Christian Scriptures on these same issues. It is nonsense to capitulate to the reasoning that quoting the Bible is imposing Judeo-Christian values upon a secular, non-Christian culture, when our American government, law, and society were founded on Christian values and the vast number of Americans identify with Christian values.

Sex Does Make a Difference

Is sex an important element in human personality? The Bible teaches, "So God created man in his own image, in the image of God he created him; male and female he created them" (Gen. 1:27).

Parents versus Child-care Centers

Should parents care for their own children, or should children be reared in "nonsexist," federally-funded child-care centers?

> Children, obey your parents in the Lord, for this is right. "Honor your father and mother"—which is the first commandment with a promise—"that it may go well with you and that you may enjoy long life on the earth."
> Fathers, do not exasperate your children; instead, bring them up in the training and instruction of the Lord. [Eph. 6:1 – 4]

> . . . train the younger women to love their husbands and children, to be self-controlled and pure, to be busy at home, to be kind, and to be subject to their husbands, so that no one will malign the word of God. [Titus 2:4 – 5]

Heterosexual Marriage As the Basis of Family Life

> . . . each man should have his own wife, and each woman her own husband. [I Cor. 7:2]

Are you married? Do not seek a divorce. [I Cor. 7:27a]

The Christian teaching about the command for a faithful and permanent heterosexual marriage as the basis for family life and child-rearing is found in numerous passages.[23]

Of course, sex *is* a basis for selecting a marriage partner.

Do not lie with a man as one lies with a woman; that is detestable [Lev. 18:22]

... God gave them over to shameful lusts. Even their women exchanged natural relations for unnatural ones. In the same way the men also abandoned natural relations with women and were inflamed with lust for one another. Men committed indecent acts with other men, and received in themselves the due penalty for their perversion. [Rom. 1:26 — 27][24]

On Male Chauvinism

Originally, the women's movement was a reaction to the undeniable truth that our culture is, in many respects, sexist. Often an unbiblical, non-Christian double standard is evident. The Bible insists that all people have equal access to a relationship with God because "there is neither Jew nor Greek, slave nor free, male nor female, for you are all one in Christ Jesus" (Gal. 3:28). But unfortunately even some Christians have wrongly and condescendingly regarded women as inferior.

In a culture that treated women unfairly, Jesus was a champion of women's rights and of their full human dignity.[25]

Sex: To Be or Not to Be?

Should there be "an end to all distinctions based on sex," as the unisex proponents would have it? Or should parents shape the sex-

23. Genesis 1 — 2; Exodus 20; Deuteronomy 24; Malachi 2:15 — 16; Matthew 5, 19; John 4, 8; Romans 1; I Corinthians 6 — 7; Ephesians 5; I Thessalonians 4; I Timothy 3; Hebrews 13:4.

24. For an extended discussion of the problems of homosexuality, see George Alan Rekers, *Growing Up Straight: What Families Need to Know about Homosexuality* (Chicago: Moody, 1982).

25. For an extended discussion of this, see Braun and Rekers, *The Christian in an Age of Sexual Eclipse*, chapter 7, "Out of the Shadows: The Woman's Role," especially pp. 152 — 155.

ual identities of their boys to masculinity and of their girls to femininity?

If we took a vote in America, I suppose the results would be like these:

Is sex a meaningful distinction for human life?

All those in favor? 90 percent.
    (Those Americans who favor Christian values.)
All those opposed? .1 percent.
    (Members of NOW).
All those abstaining? 9.9 percent.
    (Some folks always fail to vote!)

The Real Question

For the vast majority of parents, then, the question is not whether the unisex mentality is correct. They already know sex is an important distinction and they have another, more complicated question: "*How* can I shape a normal sexual identity in my child?"

That is the topic of the remaining nine chapters of this book.

2
Sexual-identity Problems in Boys and Girls

Having considered the case of Julie as a teen-ager, we are alerted to the unfortunate consequences that result if parents do not detect the childhood symptoms of sexual-identity conflict. But so far I have suggested only some of the early signs that might be detected in a home. We can get a clearer picture of where sexual-identity problems begin by taking a careful look at some basic patterns that might emerge in childhood.

Let's take a close look at the lives of four-year-old Craig and seven-year-old Becky. These cases will highlight the symptoms that concerned parents can watch for. Then I will be able to introduce the importance of the child's family background by looking at the common denominators of families whose children suffer from sexual-identity disturbances.

The Case of Craig

Craig was a four-year, eleven-month-old boy when he was referred to me ten years ago by a physician who recommended psychological treatment because Craig wanted to be a girl, not a boy.[1] Craig's father

1. G. A. Rekers and O. I. Lovaas, "Behavioral treatment of deviant sex-role behaviors in a male child," *Journal of Applied Behavior Analysis* 7 (1974): 173 – 190. This is a technical report about the case of Craig. The article is also reprinted in *Annual Review of Behavior Therapy Theory and Practice*, ed. C. M. Franks and G. T. Wilson (New York: Brunner/Mazel, 1975), chapter 25; in *Behavior Change Annual, 1974: An Aldine Annual on Psychotherapy, Counseling, and Behavior Modification*, ed. G. R. Patterson et al. (Chicago: Aldine, 1975), chapter 38.

was a construction worker and his mother was a full-time home-maker. Craig also had an eight-year-old brother and a nine-month-old sister.

Craig understood the biological difference between boys and girls. He knew that he had a boy's body, but he nevertheless insisted that he preferred to be a girl. His problem had not surfaced overnight. From the age of two, he had worn little girls' dresses whenever he could find them. Whenever he put on girls' clothes, he would search for lipstick, eyeliner, rouge, and powder to complete his feminine appearance. He enjoyed nothing more than obtaining a woman's wig to use.

If Craig could not locate a wig, he creatively used a mop or a towel on his head to imitate a woman's hair. In fact, when he could not find female clothing to play with, he would improvise with other materials. For example, he would search in his father's dresser drawer for a T-shirt that he would put on and pretend was a dress. At first his mother thought, "Good, he's trying to be like his dad now, because he wants to wear Dad's T-shirt instead of my dresses." But it wasn't long before she discovered that Craig was play-acting that he was a woman when he wore his dad's T-shirt. At other times, Craig would wrap a towel around his waist to pretend that it was a skirt.

A Rigid Role

The depth of Craig's sexual-identity confusion was apparent in his use of effeminate gestures and mannerisms. When talking, he imitated a high-pitched feminine voice, and concentrated on feminine subjects.

At the same time, Craig was unwilling to get involved in any rough-and-tumble activities with boys. He refused to play with any boy, including his own brother, no matter how quietly or gently they played. He was very fearful of getting hurt when he played with boys, and he would never defend himself if other children teased him.

Let's Play House

Instead, Craig preferred to play with girls, and with six-year-old Kelly in particular. She lived across the street from him and had many domestic toys in her garage, including baby dolls, play stoves, baby carriages, clotheslines, doll clothes, and a play ironing board. Because she had brothers, the garage also contained cars, trucks, and play building materials that could be used to "repair" things in the child-sized "house."

Many little girls like Kelly find it easier to get other little girls to play with them in their make-believe home than it is to find a little boy to play with them. The six-, seven-, and eight-year-old boys in the neighborhood were uninterested in playing house with Kelly. But Craig sought out her company. At first Kelly became excited, because she wanted to play "mommy" and have a boy play "daddy" with her.

The first time Craig came over to Kelly's miniature home in the garage, she excitedly invited, "Let's play house."

"O.K.," said Craig, "you be the daddy, and I'll be the mommy."

Kelly sighed in mild disappointment. "O.K., for a little while."

I suppose that Kelly had played so long without any cooperative boy that at this point, she resigned herself to following Craig's request to keep him interested in playing with her. Kelly was a cooperative little girl. She was accustomed to playing only with little girls her age and she was used to trading back and forth the roles of "mommy" and "daddy." Although she could play "daddy" well after all her practice, she still preferred to play "mommy."

"O.K., Craig, it's my turn to play 'mommy' now," Kelly suggested.

But Craig insisted, "No, I'm still the 'mommy' and you're the 'daddy.' "

A half-hour of play elapsed and Kelly worked up the courage to repeat, "O.K., Craig, it's my turn to play 'mommy' now. You be the 'daddy' now and I'll be the 'mommy.' "

"No sir!" exclaimed Craig. And for the rest of the time, Craig steadfastly refused to play the part of "daddy." Finally Kelly got tired of playing "daddy," and she asked Craig to go home. Craig went crying home to his mom and complained, "Kelly won't let me play the way I want to play."

There's No Place Like Home

Craig's parents had moved to a new neighborhood when he was four years old, and the family had lived in the new neighborhood only one month before all the boys refused to play with Craig. Shortly thereafter, none of the girls wanted to play with him either. This left Craig a sad, lonely, and frustrated little boy. It was not surprising, then, that Craig stayed at home with his mother most of the time. In fact, for a child his age, Craig had an overly-dependent relationship with his mother. He demanded his mother's attention almost continually, even though she had a nine-month-old baby girl to take care of.

Craig was jealous of the attention his sister received as a girl. His mother was irritated by his constant attempts to divert her attention from the baby's needs. And Craig's mother was annoyed by Craig's feminine interests. In fact, she found herself nervously smoking more and more cigarettes as she was frustrated by Craig's behavior.

But Craig was very clever in his attempts to fulfill his feminine interests. He was skilled at manipulating his mother to satisfy his desire to take on a female role. For example, on his first visit to the University Psychology Clinic to see me, Craig offered to "help mommy" by carrying her purse when she had the baby and baby bag to carry. Then Craig picked up the purse and paraded down the hall, pretending that he was the "mommy" himself. His mother had been manipulated by his offer to help, and she shook her head in frustration. "He knows that upsets me," she said.

A Clinical Note

This brief sketch of Craig illustrates a psychological disorder known as "cross-gender identification" or "sexual identity disturbance."[2] This behavior pattern in childhood is reported retrospectively by large numbers of adult male homosexuals, transsexuals, and transvestites.[3] A male homosexual is an adult who engages in sexual relations with another male. A male transsexual is a physically normal man who feels that he is a "woman trapped in a man's body" and typically asks physicians for sex-reassignment surgery and female hormones

2. A. C. Rosen, G. A. Rekers and L. R. Friar, "Theoretical and diagnostic issues in child gender disturbances," *The Journal of Sex Research* 13, no. 2 (1977): 89 – 103; G. A. Rekers and G. C. Milner, "Sexual identity disorders in childhood and adolescence," *Journal of the Florida Medical Association* 65 (1978): 962 – 964; G. A. Rekers and G. C. Milner, "How to diagnose and manage childhood sexual disorders," *Behavioral Medicine* 6, no. 4 (1979): 18 – 21; G. A. Rekers and G. C. Milner, "Early detection of sexual identity disorders," *Medical Aspects of Human Sexuality* 15, no. 11 (1981): 32EE – 32FF; G. A. Rekers, "Childhood identity disorders," *Medical Aspects of Human Sexuality* 15, no. 3 (1981): 141 – 142; G. A. Rekers and O. I. Lovaas, "Experimental analysis of cross-sex behavior in male children," *Research Relating to Children* 28 (1971): 68.

3. See a review of the literature in G. A. Rekers et al., "Child gender disturbances: A clinical rationale for intervention," *Psychotherapy: Theory, Research, and Practice* 14 (1977): 2 – 11, and A. C. Rosen, G. A. Rekers, and P. M. Bentler, "Ethical issues in the treatment of children," *Journal of Social Issues* 34, no. 2 (1978): 122 – 136.

in order to "change" his body from that of a man to that of a woman. A male transvestite is an adult man who occasionally wears dresses and women's cosmetics, often for sexual gratification, but otherwise assumes a male role in society and does not want his male sex organs removed.

The Case of Becky

A psychiatric nurse referred Becky to me for treatment at the age of seven years, eleven months.[4] The nurse had seen Becky, her two younger sisters (ages two and six), and their mother in family therapy for approximately two years. Becky's parents were divorced.

A Masculine Mimic

Throughout her childhood, Becky dressed exclusively in boys' pants and often wore cowboy boots, while consistently rejecting feminine clothing or jewelry. Her only use of cosmetics was to draw a mustache or a beard on her face. She appeared masculine in her gestures, mannerisms, and walk. She occasionally masturbated in public and rubbed her body against other girls' bodies. She often projected her voice very low so that she sounded like a man. She expressed a strong desire to be a boy and she adopted male roles in play.

Getting Along

Becky preferred the company of boys and did not interact well with other girls. Her behavior was exclusively aggressive when she was with other children. She had a very poor relationship with her six-year-old sister, who displayed a clear preference for feminine play activities.

Becky, on the other hand, displayed masculine behaviors, not only at home but also in the presence of the psychiatric nurse who had previously treated her in family therapy, and in the clinic. However, Becky apparently did not exhibit enough of these masculine behaviors in school to warrant the concern of school personnel, since no

4. G. A. Rekers and S. L. Mead, "Early intervention for female sexual identity disturbance: Self-monitoring of play behavior," *Journal of Abnormal Child Psychology* 7, no. 4 (1979): 405 – 423.

one had ever reported any significant behavioral problems to her mother. Becky's mother attributed this discrepancy to Becky's fear of her teacher, which resulted in overall subdued behavior at school.

Toys and Tomboys

My psychological testing of Becky found her to have a high IQ. I also found strong evidence of Becky's male identification. During one of the tests, in which Becky was asked which articles a stick figure would like to play with, Becky stated a preference for a razor and spontaneously added, " 'Cause I'm a boy." When Becky was asked about what the stick figure would like to be when it grew up, she said "a daddy" and added, " 'Cause if you're a daddy, you don't have babies."

Overall, Becky had a serious case of sexual-identity confusion which was similar to the backgrounds of many female homosexuals. In general, many lesbians were considered tomboys when they were young, they had opposite-sex peer groups, and they avoided typically feminine activities at the ages that most girls spent their time with other girls in girlish play.[5] Compared with heterosexual women who were also tomboys in their youth, significantly more lesbians who were tomboys also reported an aversion to playing with dolls.[6] Overall, women with sexual-identity disturbances have told psychologists that they behaved as Becky did when they were little girls. In other words, lesbians often acted more like boys than like girls when they were Becky's age.

Troubled Children

I selected the cases of Craig and Becky to illustrate extreme examples of the basic kinds of sexual-identity problems that can begin to emerge in early childhood. Don't let these extreme examples fool you into believing that only such obviously troubled children are running the risk of serious homosexual temptation as teen-agers and adults. Craig and Becky are examples of childhood patterns in full

5. See a review of the research studies in G. A. Rekers and S. L. Mead, "Female sex-role deviance: Early identification and developmental intervention," *Journal of Clinical Child Psychology* 9, no. 3 (1980): 199 – 203, cited in "Development of Social Skills," *University of Sheffield Biomedical Information Service* 1, no. 3 (March 1981): 4.

6. *Ibid.*

bloom, but many other children have some of these symptoms and may therefore face the same kind of trouble in the future.

In chapters 8 and 9 we will consider how Craig and Becky were helped to become normal children. Because children with severe problems can be helped, children with milder problems can have hope too, if parents detect the symptoms early. However, let's try to resist our curiosity about what happened to Craig and Becky. For now, let's consider some important background issues first. Let's think about the family factors related to the causes of children's sexual-identity problems.

A Study of Families

For the past twelve years, I have devoted the major portion of my professional career to the intensive study of more than 100 children and teen-agers who were identified by their pediatricians, psychologists, psychiatrists, schools, or other social agencies as having problems with their sex-role adjustment. With more than half a million dollars of support from research grants I have been carefully studying these troubled children, both boys and girls, who are three to eighteen years old.[7] In addition to conducting a careful study of these youngsters, I have also written articles about the psychological treatment that these children desperately needed.[8]

Not surprisingly, I have discovered that the family backgrounds of these young people tend to be quite a bit more troubled than those of normal children. The question has been, however, "Exactly how are these families different?"

Types of Sexual Problems

The children that I have described in these two chapters are examples of the major types of cases I have studied. Julie is an example of a teen-ager who has strong romantic attachments to

7. My clinical research has been funded by a graduate fellowship (1970 – 1972) from the National Science Foundation at the University of California at Los Angeles, by a post-doctoral fellowship (1972 – 1973) at Harvard University from the Foundations' Fund for Research in Psychiatry, and by United States Public Health Service research grants (1973 – 1980) from the National Institute of Mental Health (grant numbers MH21803, MH28240, and MH29945), the last at the Logos Research Institute, Inc.

8. Rekers et al., "Child gender disturbances"; see also G. A. Rekers, "Assessment and treatment of childhood gender problems," in *Advances in Clinical Child Psychology*, ed. Benjamin B. Lahey and Alan E. Kazdin (New York: Plenum, 1977), volume 1, chapter 7.

other girls and who suffers from a severe sexual-identity disturbance. Craig is an example of a young boy with serious problems in male role development. His childhood is very similar to the type of childhood reported by the majority of adult male homosexuals, transvestites, and transsexuals. Becky is an example of a young girl whose early childhood years are similar to those reported by adult female homosexuals and transsexuals.

Let's look at the importance of the family background of children troubled by sex-role deviations. Let's direct our attention to young children in order to illustrate the importance of family factors in early childhood adjustment to one's sex role. For the moment, let's focus on what we have learned about the families of young boys with sex-role difficulties. In other words, for the children like Craig, what do the family backgrounds tend to be like?

Family Backgrounds of Troubled Children

I did a careful study of forty-six boys like Craig who ranged in age from three to thirteen years, with an average age of seven years.[9] I was interested in the question of what factors in a family might make these boys vulnerable to problems in sex-role development.

Male Role Examples

One of the most obvious first questions had to do with whether the father was physically present in or absent from the home. If the father was present, I tried to find out what kind of relationship the biological father or the substitute father had with the boy. On the other hand, if the father was absent from the home, I was interested in studying the age of the boy at the time of his separation from his father, and I was interested in the reason for the separation from the father.

Whether or not the father was at home at the time of my study, I was also interested in whether the father had a psychiatric history. To round out my concern regarding the male role examples that these boys might have, I also recorded the number of older brothers that the boy might have.

9. G. A. Rekers et al., "Family correlates of male childhood gender disturbance," *The Journal of Genetic Psychology*, 1982, in press.

Mother's Role

I also thought it would be important to find the differences between the role that the mothers took in these families as compared with the role taken by the fathers. For this reason, I developed a Behavior Checklist for Childhood Gender Problems,[10] which asked a number of questions about the fathers, the mothers, and the everyday home environment.

Psychological Testing

I was interested in finding out how involved emotionally the troubled boy was with his mother, his father, and other family members. For this reason, I hired other psychologists to administer a Family Relations Test[11] to as many of these boys as possible.

For the first three dozen of these boys that I studied, I wanted to make the most careful psychological diagnosis possible, given the state of the art in clinical psychology. For this reason, I asked two other clinical psychologists to join me in evaluating these boys.[12] One of these clinical psychologists extensively interviewed the mother and the father of the boy, first together and then individually. He then interviewed the child extensively and administered numerous standard clinical psychological tests.

The other clinical psychologist developed a Child Behavior and Attitude Questionnaire[13] and a Child Game Participation Questionnaire[14] based upon research on normal boys and girls ranging in age from early to late childhood. Using norms based on the answers from these questionnaires, he was able to evaluate the boys with sexrole problems and to provide a psychometric diagnosis for the child.

In addition to these studies made by the other two clinical psychologists, I also interviewed the parents and the child and observed

10. G. A. Rekers, "Pathological sex-role development in boys: Behavioral treatment and assessment" (Ph.D. diss., University of California, Los Angeles, 1972).

11. E. Bene and J. Anthony, "Bene-Anthony family relations test: An objective technique for exploring emotional attitudes in children." Distributed by the National Foundation for Educational Research in England and Wales. Copyright 1957.

12. P. M. Bentler, G. A. Rekers, and A. C. Rosen, "Congruence of childhood sex-role identity and behaviour disturbances," *Child: Care, Health and Development* 5, no. 4 (1979): 267 – 284.

13. J. E. Bates, P. M. Bentler, and S. Thompson, "Measurement of deviant gender development in boys," *Child Development* 44 (1973): 591 – 598.

14. J. E. Bates and P. M. Bentler, "Play activities of normal and effeminate boys," *Developmental Psychology* 9 (1973): 20 – 27.

the child play in controlled clinic situations in which I was able to compare the child's play with the play of normal boys and girls, as well as make specific recordings of any effeminate gestures or mannerisms of the child. When I interviewed the parents, I asked questions about how work is divided at home, how decisions are made on important questions at home, the parents' approach to discipline, the patterns of support and affection expressed by each of the parents toward the boy, and also the amount of contact of each parent with the boy. This was in addition to standard questions about the child's adjustment and numerous questions about the child's own appreciation of his physical sexual status and awareness of his sexual identity.

Then all three of us, as psychologists, made a diagnosis of each boy, on a scale from one to five. A rating of one indicated the most extreme sex-role disturbance and a rating of five indicated normal sex-role adjustment.

Psychological Problems in Parents

One of the most striking results of our research had to do with the high incidence of psychological problems in the families of these disturbed boys. Of those families for whom we could obtain the information, a full two-thirds had at least one parent who had been under the extensive care of a psychiatrist, psychologist, or other mental-health professional. For 80 percent of the boys with sex-role problems, the mothers had mental-health problems. For 45 percent of these disturbed boys, the fathers had mental-health difficulties. It may be possible that these percentages are somewhat inflated because the parents who have sought psychological help for themselves might be likely to seek such treatment for their own child. But the results are so extreme as to suggest that the parents, and especially the mothers, of boys with sex-role problems have histories of serious psychological difficulties themselves.

The Boys' Fathers

Unlike the majority of children in America, we found that 67 percent of these boys with sex-role problems were not living in a home with their biological father. In fact, the biological father was absent for nearly all of the boys who had been diagnosed as having the most profoundly disturbed sex-role adjustment. In contrast, the boys with a moderate to mild sex-role adjustment problem had fathers absent in 54 percent of the cases. Our statistical tests of these data demonstrated our scientific findings. The more profoundly disturbed the boy is in sex-role adjustment, the more likely he is to be separated from his biological father.

On the average, we found that the boys were three-and-one-half years old at the time the father left the home. Eighty percent of the boys were five years of age or younger when their separation from their father occurred.

In 82 percent of the cases, the parents were separated or divorced. Only one of the fathers was dead, and in two cases the mothers had never legally married.

Fathers or Father Substitutes

For boys whose fathers had left, it is always possible that the mother has remarried so that the boys have father substitutes who can serve as an example of a male role. We found that 37 percent of these boys with sex-role problems had no adult male role example present in the home. This means that more than a third of the boys had neither a biological father nor a father substitute living at home with them.

This is a much higher rate of male role absence in the home than we find in the general population. According to available United States census figures,[15] only 11.9 percent of all white children in the United States live with their mothers, without the benefit of a father or a father substitute in the home.

Once again, we separated these boys with sex-role problems into two groups: the most severely disturbed boys and the less severely disturbed boys. Making this simple grouping, we found that 75 percent of the most severely disturbed boys had neither the biological father nor a father substitute living at home with them, whereas 21 percent of the less severely disturbed boys had neither the biological father nor a father substitute living with them. (Once again, our statistical tests demonstrated that this was a scientific finding, not likely due to chance occurrence.)

15. U. S. Bureau of the Census, *Statistical Abstracts of the United States: 1978* (Washington, DC: U. S. Department of Commerce, 1978).

Psychologically Remote Fathers

Tragically, we found that when a father figure was present physically, he was often psychologically remote from the rest of the family. In other words, the father was living in the same house, but he was not very involved emotionally with the other family members. In fact, for the boys with sex-role problems who were fortunate enough to have a biological father or father substitute living in the home, fully 60 percent of those father figures were found to be psychologically distant and remote from the other family members. This means that only about one in four of these boys with a sex-role problem had what might be described as a normal, close relationship with a father or a father substitute.

Older Brothers

It is possible that boys without a father can learn about the male role by the example of their older brothers. When we scrutinized our findings on this question, fewer than half of the boys had an older brother, and the results suggested a trend where the most severely gender-disturbed boys were less likely to have an older brother as an example of a male role than were the less severely disturbed boys.

Missing Male Models

We discovered a consistent picture which emerged from all the facts that we collected about these boys' families. As compared with most boys in America, these boys with severe sex-role problems are much less likely to have a father figure living in the home with them, and even when the father figure is present he tends to be psychologically remote from the boy. The boys with the most severe sex-role problems are much less likely to have a good male role example living in their own home than are the other boys with sex-role problems.

Mothers in Power

In those families that did have a father present, what was the family interaction like? On this question, we have some accumulated clinical experience rather than research data. This means that we can only make a tentative description of what these families are like. Our clinical records show that in the families of disturbed boys, the mothers held the balance of power with regard to financial decisions in more than half of the families. The mothers also held the balance of power with regard to decisions concerning the children in three-fourths of these families.

Our clinical records also show that in the majority of cases, the boys with sex-role problems typically go to the mother rather than to the father for sympathy. They are more likely to object being separated from their mother than their father, and they are more likely to cling to the mother than to the father. It also appears that the mothers rather than the fathers are somewhat more likely to be the ones to discipline the child when both parents are present.

Feelings for Fathers

Based on use of the Family Relations Test, our clinical record shows that the older boys with sex-role difficulties are more likely than normal children to endorse statements such as, "I wish this person [the father] would go away," "this person is not very patient," and "this person can make one feel very angry."

In conclusion, we have discovered that boys with serious sex-role disturbances live in families in which a male role model is usually absent or inadequate. In many cases, the boy did not have a father, a father substitute, or an older brother to look up to as an example of acceptable male behavior. In cases where a father or father substitute did live in the same home, he was usually psychologically remote from the boy. This means that these boys with sex-role disturbances did not have, in most cases, a male role model to identify with. In fact, the most severely disturbed boys had no father figure at home.

It was the less severely disturbed boys whose fathers were psychologically remote from the family if they were present at all. This means these fathers were not involved in making important family decisions and did not have affectionate, helping relationships with their sons.

This evidence from these clinical cases suggest that the father's role in the family is critically important for the development of sex-role adjustment.[16]

16. S. L. Mead and G. A. Rekers, "The role of the father in normal psychosexual development," *Psychological Reports* 45 (1979): 923 – 931; Rekers et al., "Family correlates."

Parents of Children with Sexual-identity Problems

A few recent studies of the fathers of children with sexual-identity problems report findings similar to those of my own study. These studies find the same kind of family factors that are found in clinical studies of adult homosexuals and transsexuals.

Parental Problems

One investigation of children with sexual-identity problems[17] found that the fathers of transsexual boys are not only passive but also are sometimes effeminate themselves. In eight out of the nine cases in the study, the father was often away from the home during the early years of the boy's life. When the father was present, he was found to be psychologically distant from the other family members.

The father's absence or psychological distance means that these boys did not have an adequate male role model in their homes. This interfered with their identifying with the male role themselves. In addition, the mothers and sons developed an excessively close relationship, which could not be corrected by a father because the father was either absent or very remote from family life. Although divorce was uncommon in this group, the relationship between the mother and the father was often distant and unhappy.

This study suggested that the family backgrounds of male transsexuals differ from the family backgrounds of male homosexuals in several respects. For both male transsexuals and homosexuals, the mothers tended to be domineering and overprotective. But the mothers of transsexuals were particularly competitive with males during their own childhood and early adolescence. The mothers of transsexual sons were also more likely to encourage a "blissful closeness" with their sons than were the mothers of male homosexuals. Although the mother-father relationship was unhappy and strained, divorce was uncommon for parents of transsexual sons. In contrast, the parents of homosexuals were more likely to get a divorce.

17. R. J. Stoller, "Parental influences in male transsexualism," in *Transsexualism and Sex Reassignment*, ed. Richard Green and John Money (Baltimore: Johns Hopkins, 1969), pp. 153 – 169.

Family Sex-role Reversals

In another study of thirty-eight boys who wore girls' dresses, said that they desired to be girls, and preferred feminine activities, a similar set of findings emerged.[18] In these boys with sex-role disturbances, there appeared to be no male model during the boys' first few years of life. In addition, the mother tended to dominate the family. The fathers rejected their sons at an early age and both parents were indifferent to encouraging masculine behaviors in their sons. In some cases the parents even encouraged feminine behaviors in their sons.

In this group of boys, one-third of them lost a father before the age of four, compared with only eight percent of most boys in the United States. As was true in other studies, even when the fathers were physically present in the home, they were often psychologically distant from other family members.

About three-fourths of the boys preferred their mother over their father, and only seven percent preferred their father over their mother. In contrast, normal boys tend not to show such a strong preference for either parent, and if they do prefer one parent they are less likely to prefer their mother over their father.

Unmasculine Fathers

Finally, another study of the families of boys with sexual-identity disturbances also found the fathers to be psychologically distant from the family.[19] This study pointed out that the fathers of the disturbed boys did not take upon themselves any significant role in policy-setting in the family. In this case the fathers were nominally loving and not openly rejecting or punitive. But these fathers provided very little structured discipline for their sons and they were reported to be quiet and peripheral in their family involvement.

Another study[20] also found the fathers of effeminate boys to be aloof and psychologically absent from the home, as well as uninvolved with decisionmaking in the family. These men were ineffective as both fathers and husbands. But in contrast with the study I just

18. Richard Green, *Sexual Identity Conflict in Children and Adults* (New York: Basic Books, 1974).

19. A. C. Rosen and J. Teague, "Case studies in development of masculinity and femininity in male children," *Psychological Reports* 34 (1974): 971 – 983.

20. W. McCord, J. McCord, and P. Verden, "Family relationship and sexual deviance in lower-class adolescents," *International Journal of Social Psychiatry* 8 (1962): 165 – 179.

described, these fathers tended to be especially punishing and they either ignored their boys or openly expressed their hatred for their sons.

There appears to be only one study[21] that has examined effeminate boys and not found this general pattern with regard to the father-son and mother-son relationships.

How Fathers Make a Difference

So far we have been considering the results of clinical experience with children with sexual-identity problems. These findings are similar to those of studies about the childhood and adolescence of adult homosexuals and transsexuals.[22] But there is yet another set of evidence which needs to be described to every serious parent. This is the extensive research about the effects on children when a father is absent from the home, and the studies on the characteristics of fathers that lead to normal sexual-identity development.

21. B. Zuger, "The role of familial factors in persistent effeminate behavior in boys," *American Journal of Psychiatry* 126 (1970): 1167 – 1170.

22. L. B. Apperson and W. G. McAdoo, "Parental factors in the childhood of homosexuals," *Journal of Abnormal Psychology* 73 (1968): 201 – 206; Alan P. Bell and Martin S. Weinberg, *Homosexualities: A Study of Diversity Among Men and Women* (New York: Simon and Schuster, 1978); E. Bene, "On the genesis of male homosexuality: An attempt at clarifying the role of the parents," *British Journal of Psychiatry* 111 (1965): 803 – 813; Irving Bieber et al., *Homosexuality: A Psychoanalytic Study* (New York: Basic Books, 1962); D. G. Brown, "Homosexuality and family dynamics," *Bulletin of the Menninger Clinic* 27 (1963): 227 – 232; Frank M. duMas, *Gay Is Not Good* (Nashville: Thomas Nelson, 1979); R. B. Evans, "Childhood parental relationships of homosexual men," *Journal of Consulting and Clinical Psychology* 33 (1969): 129 – 135; E. Hooker, "Male homosexuality in the Rorschach," *Journal of Projective Techniques* 22 (1958): 33 – 53; E. Hooker, "What is a criterion?" *Journal of Projective Techniques* 23 (1959): 278 – 281; E. Hooker, "Parental relations and male homosexuality in patient and non-patient samples," *Journal of Consulting and Clinical Psychology* 33 (1969): 140 – 142; C. H. Jonas, "An objective approach to the personality and environment in homosexuality," *Psychiatric Quarterly* 18 (1944): 626 – 641; J. Nash and F. Hayes, "The parental relationships of male homosexuals: Some theoretical issues and a pilot study," *Australian Journal of Psychology* 17 (1965): 35 – 43; Marcel T. Saghir and Eli Robins, *Male and Female Homosexuality: A Comprehensive Investigation* (Baltimore: Williams and Wilkins, 1973); Charles W. Socarides, *The Overt Homosexual* (New York: Grune and Stratton, 1968); W. G. Stephan, "Parental relationships and early social experience of activist male homosexuals and male heterosexuals," *Journal of Abnormal Psychology* 82 (1973): 506 – 513; Lewis M. Terman and Catherine C. Miles, *Sex and Personality: Studies in Masculinity and Femininity* (1936; reprint ed. New York: Russell and Russell, 1968); D. J. West, "Parental relationships in male homosexuality," *International Journal of Social Psychiatry* 5 (1959): 85 – 97.

3

When Fathers or Mothers
Neglect Their Roles

Many different factors are involved in the long-term sexual adjustment of children and in their development of a secure sexual identity as a male or a female. The child can be influenced by his father, mother, brothers and sisters, friends, by television, magazines, teachers in school, and people at church. In fact, all of the child's major experiences in life can have an influence on his or her sexual-identity development.

In the child's first five years of life, however, the parents are usually the most significant influences on the child. After age five, the other factors of family, school, church, media, and society become primary influences on the child's decisions. A child makes many small daily decisions which add up to his or her final, adult sexual adjustment. The choices made by parents and the choices made by the child and teen-ager will result in either a normal heterosexual adjustment for the child or a sexual deviation of some sort.

Should parents choose the unisex style of childrearing, or are there reasons why mothers and fathers should take different roles?

Results of Child-development Research

According to research findings, the role of the father in the family is critically important for many different aspects of childrearing. It is not sufficient to say that two parents are better than one, because there is a unique advantage for the child in having both a female parent and a male parent. As a male, the father makes a unique contribution to the childrearing of either a son or a daughter. While it is desirable for the father to be actively involved in rearing a child for the social, emotional, and spiritual needs of the child, I will focus my attention here on the unique contribution that the father makes to the sexual identity of his children.

One of the most important roles that the father has in the family is to promote the development of a normal heterosexual role and normal sexual identity in his children. The father is more actively involved in heterosexual role development of his sons and daughters than the mother is.[1] The father usually fulfills an active role in the family, as compared with the expressive role of the mother.[2] The father is, therefore, more involved than the mother is in preparing the children for their roles in society, including masculine roles for his sons and feminine roles for his daughters.

Effects of the Father's Absence on Masculine Development of Boys

Unfortunately, fathers are often absent from the home due to a variety of reasons such as separation, divorce, death, or military service. A number of research studies have been conducted on the question of whether a fatherless home has a detrimental influence on the development of boys.

One study found that young boys whose fathers were absent from the home were more likely to exhibit more feminine ways of thinking, low masculinity, dependence, and either less aggression or exaggeratedly masculine behaviors than were boys whose fathers were present.[3] Other studies have also reported negative effects on the sex-role development of boys that are associated with the father's absence. Boys who were separated from their fathers during their preschool

1. B. I. Fagot, "Sex differences in toddler's behavior and parental reaction," *Developmental Psychology* 10 (1974): 554 – 558; J. Z. Rubin, F. J. Provenzano, and Z. Luria, "The eye of the beholder: parents' views on the sex of newborns," *American Journal of Orthopsychiatry* 44 (1974): 512 – 519.

2. David B. Lynn, *The Father: His Role in Child Development* (Monterey, CA: Brooks/Cole, 1974).

3. L. Carlsmith, "Effect of early father-absence on scholastic aptitude," *Harvard Educational Review* 34 (1964): 3 – 21; Lois H. Stolz et al., *Father Relations of War-Born Children: The Effect of Post-War Adjustment of Fathers on the Behavior and Personality of First Children Born While Fathers Were at War* (1954; reprint ed., Westport, CT: Greenwood, 1969).

years were more often called sissies than were boys who had not been separated from their fathers.[4]

A group of forty-one male orphans who had been reared exclusively by women from six months to five years of age were studied.[5] A battery of psychological tests found these boys to score in the feminine direction as compared with a control group of boys who lived in homes with fathers. When the orphan boys were five years old, half of the group were moved to cottages where a married couple took care of the children. The orphan boys who lived with the father figure later had masculinity scores that were higher than those of the other orphans, who had remained in the totally feminine environment. However, it was found that both groups of orphans still remained relatively low on their masculinity scores as compared with the control group who had fathers present from earliest infancy.

In studies that compare boys with fathers to boys without fathers, the fatherless boys are more likely to be perceived as effeminate than are the boys with fathers.[6] When fatherless boys become adults, they have less successful heterosexual adjustment than do males who grew up in homes with a father.[7] Therefore, all these studies indicate that the absence of the father can have a detrimental effect upon normal heterosexual role development in boys.

Another body of evidence has suggested that sex-role problems in boys with serious sexual-identity problems are correlated with either the physical absence or the psychological distance of the father from the young boy.[8] These studies of sex-role disturbances in boys parallel the findings of the other studies I have just reviewed. We may conclude, then, that the absence of the father tends to have a detrimental effect on the normal masculine role development of boys. We may also conclude that the father is very important in fostering a normal heterosexual role development in his boy. This is not to say

4. Stolz et al., *Father Relations of War-Born Children*.

5. J. Nash, "The father in contemporary culture and current psychological literature," *Child Development* 36 (1965): 261–297.

6. G. R. Bach, "Father-fantasies and father-typing in father-separated children," *Child Development* 17 (1946): 63–80; W. N. Stephens, "Judgment by social workers on boys and mothers in fatherless families," *Journal of Genetic Psychology* 99 (1961): 59–64.

7. R. F. Winch, "The relation between the loss of a parent and progress in courtship," *Journal of Social Psychology* 29 (1949): 51–56.

8. A. C. Rosen and J. Teague, "Case studies in development of masculinity and femininity in male children," *Psychological Reports* 34 (1974): 971–983.

that the father is absolutely essential in order to rear a normal boy
(there are cases in which widows, for example, have successfully
reared normal boys), but as a general finding, the normal sex-role
development of a boy usually depends upon the presence of the
father or a father figure in early childhood.

When Does the Father's Absence Have
Its Biggest Effect?

Overall, the younger the age of the boy when the father departs,
the more harmful is the impact on the boy's heterosexual role development. One psychological research study[9] found no difference in
the sex-role behaviors of boys whose fathers have left the home after
they were five years old as compared with boys whose fathers were
present all during childhood. But this same study found strong effects
of the father's absence if the father left during the boy's first four
years of life. Therefore, the younger the boy is when the father leaves,
the more profound the effects will be on the boy's sex-role development.

Different symptoms at different ages. The boy's age at the time of
separation from the father not only is related to how strong the effect
is on the boy, but also may determine the *kind* of effect that the
father's absence will have on the boy. If the father is separated from
an infant or preschooler, the boy is likely to develop a tendency
toward effeminacy. But if the separation from the father occurs during the years just before adolescence, the effect is likely an exaggerated pattern of masculine behaviors.[10] The son is much more likely
to display an exaggerated masculine aggressiveness if the father leaves
the home when the boy is between the ages of six and twelve.[11]

The same problem, with different symptoms. If the father leaves
the boy before the age of five, effeminate behavior is likely to develop,
whereas if the father leaves between the ages of six and twelve,
hypermasculine problem behavior may result. At first glance, these
opposite results may appear to be puzzling. But one way to under-

9. E. M. Hetherington, "Effects of paternal absence on sex-typed behaviors in Negro and
white preadolescent males," *Journal of Personality and Social Psychology* 4 (1966): 87 — 91.

10. J. W. Santrock, "Effects of father absence on sex-typed behaviors in male children:
Reason for the absence and age at onset of the absence," *Journal of Genetic Psychology* 130
(1977): 3 — 10.

11. J. L. McCord, W. L. McCord, and E. Thurber, "Some effects of paternal absence on
male children," *Journal of Abnormal and Social Psychology* 64 (1962): 361 — 369.

stand these opposite effects is to remember that normal heterosexual role development is best fostered when the father is present throughout the entire childhood of the boy. When the father is absent, the boy is likely to suffer an inadequate masculine role development. There are two kinds of inadequate masculine role development: deviation in the feminine direction, and deviation in the exaggerated, hypermasculine direction. Therefore, unusual amounts of effeminate behavior in a boy are only one kind of problem in male sex-role development.

Excessive aggression and exaggerated masculine behavior are also evidence of an inadequate masculine role development.[12] The older boy without a father may have trouble in mastering what is appropriate masculine behavior, and in the process he may overcompensate for the loss of the father by acting in extremely "masculine" ways. For example, the boy may become belligerent, uncontrollable, insensitive to the feelings of others, and aggressive to the point of interpersonal violence. None of these are desirable masculine qualities, although they can be recognized as abnormal attempts to achieve a secure masculine image.

Researchers therefore found that in the absence of a father, some boys (particularly younger ones) develop excessive feminine characteristics as a reflection of an inadequate male role development. Older boys who lose their father are more likely to reveal their inadequate heterosexual role development by being exaggeratedly "masculine" as an unfortunate result of compensating for the loss of the father.

As a footnote, it should be pointed out that the research on heterosexual development is more complex than I can describe here, in that different aspects of heterosexual role development have been studied, including sex-role preference, sex-role orientation, and sex-role adoption. Father absence has its strongest effect on sex-role orientation, which is defined as the conscious or unconscious sense of basic maleness or femaleness in the child.[13]

---

12. Charles C. Harrington, *Errors in Sex-Role Behavior in Teen-age Boys* (New York: Teachers College Press, 1970).

13. H. B. Biller, "A multiaspect investigation of masculine development in kindergarten age boys," *Genetic Psychology Monographs* 78 (1968): 89 – 138; C. T. Drake and D. McDugall, "Effects of the absence of the father and other male models on the development of boys' sex roles," *Developmental Psychology* 13 (1977): 537 – 538.

Does the Reason for the Father's Absence
Make a Difference?

There has been very little research that would answer this question. However, a recent study[14] found that boys whose parents are divorced are more likely to be aggressive than those whose fathers are dead.

Can the Effects of the Father's Absence
Be Counteracted?

The presence of a father substitute has generally been found to counteract, somewhat, the effects of the father's absence on a child's development.[15] One research study found that black preschool boys were more feminine, more dependent, and less aggressive if their father was absent, as compared with other boys who had fathers present in their home. However, a group of boys who had father substitutes were found to be less dependent than the boys with no fathers or father substitutes.[16] But a father substitute may not be quite as effective as one continuous father in some cases, as suggested by another psychological study which failed to find a compensating effect by the presence of a father substitute.[17]

Even if a father or father substitute is not present in the home, there is another factor which has been found to lessen the effect of the father's absence. Research studies have identified this other factor as a positive attitude toward the father by the mother of the boy, as well as her positive attitude toward men in general.[18] This shows that the potential negative effects of the father's absence on the masculine role development of boys is not a simple thing. We must take into account other factors, such as the possibility that other male role models may be present for the boy and the fact that a mother may be able to compensate for the effects if she has positive attitudes toward men and treats her boy with respect for his masculinity.

14. Santrock, "Effects of father absence."

15. G. P. Matthews, "Father-absence and the development of masculine identification in black preschool males," *Dissertation Abstracts International* 37, no. 3-A (1976): 1458; G. Sutton-Smith, B. G. Rosenberg, and F. Landy, "Father-absence effects in families of different sibling compositions," *Child Development* 38 (1968): 1213 — 1221.

16. J. W. Santrock, "Paternal absence, sex typing, and identification," *Developmental Psychology* 2 (1970): 264 — 272.

17. Drake and McDugall, "Effects of the absence of the father."

18. H. B. Biller and R. M. Baum, "Father-absence, perceived maternal behavior, and masculinity of school boys," *Developmental Psychology* 4 (1971): 178 — 181; Matthews, "Father absence and the development of masculine identification."

Effects of the Father's Absence on Feminine Development of Girls

There are relatively fewer research studies that have dealt with the effects of the father's absence on the development of the daughter than there are studies about sons. But the few studies available suggest that the father's absence is less devastating to the sex-role development of girls as compared with boys. In fact, some studies[19] have not found any differences in the heterosexual role development of girls in father-absent as compared with father-present homes. But more recent studies have found some subtle, complex effects of the father's absence on the development of girls.

As was the case with boys, the negative consequences of a fatherless home can have different effects, depending on the reason for the father's absence. In a research study of a group of adolescent females, the girls were found to be inhibited in their interactions with males in general if the father had died.[20] On the other hand, if the parents were divorced, the girls were overly responsive to males and displayed early and inappropriate sexual behaviors. Sophisticated research studies are therefore finding that the absence of the father can have a debilitating effect on the sex-role development of girls.

What Characteristics of a Father Contribute to Normal Heterosexual Role Development in Children?

Earlier research studies focused on the differences in children in homes with fathers as compared to homes without fathers. More recent studies have concentrated on which of the father's characteristics make a difference in the heterosexual role development of his children.[21]

19. Santrock, "Paternal absence"; Winch, "Loss of a parent and progress in courtship."
20. E. M. Hetherington, "Effects of father-absence on personality development in adolescent daughters," *Developmental Psychology* 7 (1972): 313 – 326.
21. H. B. Biller, "The father and personality development: Paternal deprivation and sex-role development," in *The Role of the Father in Child Development*, ed. Michael E. Lamb (New York: Wiley, 1976), pp. 89 – 156; Michael E. Lamb, ed., *The Role of the Father in Child Development*; Lynn, *The Father: His Role in Child Development*; D. B. Lynn, "Fathers and sex-role development," *Family Coordinator* 25 (1976): 403 – 409; G. A. Rekers et al., "Family correlates of male childhood gender disturbance," *The Journal of Genetic Psychology*, 1982, in press; S. L. Mead and G. A. Rekers, "The role of the father in normal psycho-sexual development," *Psychological Reports* 45 (1979): 923 – 931; Rosen and Teague, "Development of masculinity and femininity."

Warm, Affectionate Fathers

The degree of the father's active, involved affection toward his children is the most important factor related to normal heterosexual role development in his child. Research studies have shown that the father who is affectionate and involved with his child is most likely to foster masculinity in his son. Appropriate sex-role development has been correlated with father-son interactions which can be characterized as warm, nurturant, and affectionate.[22] The warm affection of the father was more important than the father's actual, literal encouragement of masculine behaviors, and it was also more important than the extent to which the father himself was masculine as opposed to feminine. Many different studies have shown that appropriately masculine boys come from families with fathers who are affectionate, nurturant, and actively involved in childrearing.[23] Boys are more likely to identify with their fathers if their father is rewarding and affectionate toward them than if the fathers are not.[24]

At the same time, normal feminine role development in girls is also related to a warm, nurturant relationship with the mother. The father's influence on daughters is different from the father's influence on sons. The normal feminine girls tend to have highly masculine fathers who encourage feminine behaviors in their daughters.

Quality of Father-Son Relationship

Other characteristics of fathers have been considered important to the appropriate and heterosexual role development of children. The results of research studies testing these ideas have not provided many absolute conclusions. For example, research has not found heterosexual role development dependent upon how similar a boy feels he is to his father or how similar a girl feels that she is to her

22. P. H. Mussen and E. Rutherford, "Parent-child relation and parental personality in relation to young children's sex-role preferences," *Child Development* 34 (1963): 589 – 607.

23. E. M. Hetherington, "A developmental study of the effects of sex of the dominant parent on sex-role preference, identification, and imitation in children," *Journal of Personality and Social Psychology* 2 (1965): 188 – 194; Lamb, *Role of the Father in Child Development*; P. H. Mussen and L. Distler, "Child rearing antecedents of masculine identification in kindergarten boys," *Child Development* 31 (1960): 89 – 100; D. E. Payne and P. H. Mussen, "Parent-child relations and father identification among adolescent boys," *Journal of Abnormal and Social Psychology* 52 (1956): 358 – 362.

24. Mussen and Distler, "Child rearing antecedents"; P. H. Mussen and L. Distler, "Masculinity, identification, and father-son relationships," *Journal of Abnormal and Social Psychology* 59 (1959): 350 – 356.

mother.[25] Some fathers are more available than others to spend time with their boys, but better masculine role development has not been found for the boys whose fathers are more available.[26] If the father is living in the home and is usually available, it has been concluded that the quality of the father-son relationship may be more important than the number of interactions that they have.[27]

Father's Example

Dr. Masters of the well-known Masters and Johnson team described the importance of models for sex education:

> There is nothing that teaches sex half so much as Pop patting Mom's fanny as he walks by her in the kitchen. Obviously, she loves it, and the kids watch and say "Boy that's for me."[28]

John W. Drakeford points out, "But what if instead of seeing Daddy make an affectionate gesture towards Mother, he sees brutality, force, sex without love, and the callous exploitation of women, won't he identify with these?"[29]

Father's Assertion of Leadership

The different amounts of power assumed by the father and the mother in a family can also influence the heterosexual role development of children.[30] Generally speaking, the child is likely to identify with the parent who is the leader in the household. Boys from homes in which the mother asserted herself as the leader exhibited more feminine sex-role preferences than did boys from homes in which the father was leader. However, the sex-role preferences of girls were not influenced by whether the mother or father asserted leadership.[31]

25. S. Gray, "Perceived similarity to parents and adjustment," *Child Development* 30 (1959): 91 – 107.

26. M. Reis and D. Gold, "Relation of paternal availability to problem solving and sex-role orientation in young boys," *Psychological Reports* 40 (1977): 823 – 829.

27. Biller, "The father and personality development"; F. Earls, "The fathers (not the mothers): Their importance and influence with infants and young children," *Psychiatry* 39 (1976): 209 – 226.

28. As quoted by John W. Drakeford and Jack Hamm, *Pornography: The Sexual Mirage* (Nashville: Thomas Nelson, 1973), pp. 143 – 144.

29. *Ibid.*, p. 144.

30. Hetherington, "Developmental study of the effects of sex."

31. *Ibid.*

In another research study, children were asked who they wanted to be like when they grew up.[32] In homes where the mother was the leading parent, there were many boys who chose to be a female when they grew up. At the same time, in homes in which the mother asserted leadership, the girls were likely to want to be a male.

It was also found that in homes led by assertive mothers, both girls and boys were likely to say that they disliked the opposite sex (as determined by sociometric ratings). Also, these girls and boys were frequently disliked by the opposite sex. These effects are not always observed, as reported by another study which did not find power distribution of the family to be related to some measures of sex typing in children.[33]

Father's Leadership Plus Affection

Clearly then, the father's assertion of leadership has a better effect on the heterosexual role development of both the boys and the girls than does the mother's assertion of leadership. When the mother asserts dominance, studies show that the sex-role orientation of the boys tends to be feminine and that of the girls tends to be masculine. Earlier, I reviewed the evidence which showed that the father's affection and nurturance toward the sons is very important to their masculine development. Other studies have shown that the father who both asserts leadership *and* is nurturant is more likely than the father who is remote to have sons who are masculine in their heterosexual role development.[34] In addition, there is evidence that suggests that effects of the father's leadership are expressed in the homes in which the father is also nurturant.[35]

Some of the most important factors, then, for the child's heterosexual role development are the affection and leadership of the father in the home. Additional studies have found that the father's ability to set limits for his sons is related to greater masculinity in boys if the father is also a nurturant and affectionate person.[36]

32. L. W. Hoffman, "The father's role in the family and the child's peer-group adjustment," *Merrill-Palmer Quarterly* 7 (1961): 97 − 105.

33. J. M. Greenstein, "Father characteristics and sex typing," *Journal of Personality and Social Psychology* 3 (1966): 271 − 277.

34. Lynn, *The Father: His Role in Child Development.*

35. E. M. Hetherington and J. L. Deur, "The effects of father absence on child development," *Young Children* 26 (1971): 233 − 248.

36. Biller, "The father and personality development"; Lamb, *The Role of the Father in Child Development.*

Father Failure and the Family

I have been focusing on the critical influence that the father has on the heterosexual role development of children. Of course, no single cause is likely to explain everything about sex-role development because such development can be influenced not only by the father, but also by the mother, the peer group, the brothers and sisters, the media, the school, the church, and in fact any institution or person in society with whom the child comes in contact. Nevertheless, the parents are the most significant influences in the earliest years of the child's life, and it is during those early years that sexual identity and role development are normally established.[37] Research studies have also shown that the father (rather than the mother) is the parent who is more actively involved in the heterosexual role development of the children.

Fathers Who Abandon Their Families

We have seen that the father's absence from the home can result in serious problems in heterosexual role development, especially for boys. Even if the father is present but psychologically distant or absent from the child, negative side effects in the child's development can occur.[38] Substitute father figures can help somewhat to overcome the detrimental influence of the father's absence, and the mother's positive attitude toward males can also compensate for the fatherless home.

The Needed Father Role

We have seen that the type of father who fosters normal heterosexual role development is one who is affectionate, nurturant, and actively involved with his children. In addition to being affectionate, the father who asserts leadership, is active in making family decisions, and sets firm and reasonable limits for the child also contributes to the best heterosexual role development in his children.

Family Fragmentation

Unfortunately, the role of the father in the family may be quickly changing in today's American society. The nature of the father's role

37. John Money and Anke A. Ehrhardt, *Man and Woman, Boy and Girl: Differentiation and Dimorphism of Gender Identity from Conception to Maturity* (Baltimore: Johns Hopkins, 1973).

38. Rosen and Teague, "Development of masculinity and femininity"; Rekers et al., "Family correlates."

for children of the future, and the consequences of changes in the family structure will have profound influences on the sexual identity and sex-role development of children. The increase in the number of fatherless homes that has been occurring in recent years may result in larger numbers of sexual-identity problems in children.

At the same time, there has been another trend of women being employed outside the home. Research studies indicate that the child-rearing tasks are being shifted to group child-care centers and temporary babysitters. By and large, fathers are not stepping into the vacuum created by the mother's absence from the home. In cases where the father does increase participation in childrearing, it has been suggested that the differences in the mother's and father's role in the family may become blurred as the father becomes involved in historically feminine roles.[39] This may result in greater difficulty for children to distinguish between proper male and female roles.

The Judeo-Christian Teaching

We have seen that the unisex notion of childrearing is *not* supported by the wealth of child-development research on the father's and mother's influence upon sexual-identity formation in boys and girls. The unisex idea is an unwarranted and biased viewpoint which is harmful to children and family life. We may properly refer to this notion, therefore, as the unisex myth.

The unisex myth is based upon a relativistic, humanistic world view. This is a viewpoint in opposition to the Judeo-Christian heritage of Western civilization.[40]

In fact, the results of modern child-development research on mothering and fathering are compatible with the Judeo-Christian teaching of Scripture.

> Now I want you to realize that the head of every man is Christ, and the head of the woman is man, and the head of Christ is God. [I Cor. 11:3]

39. L. W. Hoffman, "Changes in family roles, socialization, and sex differences," *American Psychologist* 32 (1977): 644 – 657.

40. See Michael Braun and George Alan Rekers, *The Christian in an Age of Sexual Eclipse* (Wheaton, IL: Tyndale, 1981), chapter 2, "The Rhetoric of Revolt: The Sexual Propaganda of Humanism," and the epilogue, "A Defense Without Apology"; G. A. Rekers, "Can the university alleviate anti-family hedonism?" *Independent University Journal* 1 (January 17, 1980):5.

Wives, submit to your husbands as to the Lord. For the husband is the head of the wife as Christ is the head of the church, his body, of which he is the Savior. Now as the church submits to Christ, so also wives should submit to their husbands in everything.

Husbands, love your wives, just as Christ loved the church and gave himself up for her. . . .

. . . each one of you also must love his wife as he loves himself, and the wife must respect her husband. [Eph. 5:22 – 25, 33]

Wives, submit to your husbands, as is fitting in the Lord.

Husbands, love your wives and do not be harsh with them.

Children, obey your parents in everything, for this pleases the Lord.

Fathers, do not embitter your children, or they will become discouraged. [Col. 3:18 – 21]

Wives, in the same way be submissive to your husbands so that, if any of them do not believe the word, they may be won over without talk by the behavior of their wives, when they see the purity and reverence of your lives. Your beauty should not come from outward adornment, such as braided hair and the wearing of gold jewelry and fine clothes. Instead, it should be that of your inner self, the unfading beauty of a gentle and quiet spirit, which is of great worth in God's sight. For this is the way the holy women of the past who put their hope in God used to make themselves beautiful. They were submissive to their own husbands, like Sarah, who obeyed Abraham and called him her master. You are her daughters if you do what is right and do not give way to fear.

Husbands, in the same way be considerate as you live with your wives, and treat them with respect as the weaker partner and as heirs with you of the gracious gift of life, so that nothing will hinder your prayers. [I Peter 3:1 – 7]

Scripture teaches that men are to assume a protective, nonexploitative role toward women (I Thess. 4:4 – 5; I Tim. 5:1 – 2; I Peter 3:7). Fathers are forbidden to be harsh with their children, and are to be loving toward them (Luke 11:13; Eph. 6:4). The man is to be in authority in the home (I Cor. 11), but in a loving way (John 15:12; I Peter 3:7; I John 2:10; 4:10). The woman is to be submissive to her husband (I Cor. 11; Eph. 5; I Peter 2:21—3:1) and therefore not the dominant force in the nuclear family. This biblical teaching parallels the outcome of the child-development research, which describes the best kind of home environment for children to develop normal sexual identities.

Therefore, the traditional difference in the desired roles for mothers and fathers in childrearing is supported by recent child-development research as well as by the Judeo-Christian heritage of Western culture, as derived from the Bible. In comparison, the unisex myth is discredited by contemporary research, and should be soundly rejected by all parents concerned for the welfare of their children.

Part **TWO**

Crimes Against Families

In my ten-year career as a psychologist, I have, from time to time, found myself facing a judge with my right hand upheld, promising to tell "the truth, the whole truth, and nothing but the truth, so help me God." Part of my professional work has been to serve as an expert psychological witness in a number of important trials.

In one case, my specialized background in sexual-identity development in children was the reason I was asked to perform psychological evaluations of each member of a family in which an openly-acknowledged and self-proclaimed bisexual mother sued her husband for divorce and for the custody of her three preschool daughters. This trial was hotly contested and widely publicized across the nation. The mother's case was supported by "gay" activist groups who hoped to set a legal precedent for placing children in the custody of an openly-practicing homosexual parent.

After interviewing and testing the family members, I was called to court to testify about my psychological findings. The attorneys asked me question after question for several hours while I was on the witness stand. They asked me questions such as the following:

Would the daughters' sexual-identity development be jeopardized
    if they were placed in the custody of this openly-acknowledged
    bisexual mother?

51

Would living with their mother make it likely that these little girls
would grow up to be bisexual or homosexual?

Is the mother or the father, in this case, more likely to provide a
stable home environment for the daughters?

Is this mother psychologically disturbed?

Is homosexuality abnormal?

The next two chapters describe some of the details of this case in
order to reveal what happens to a family when a parent consistently
carries out the unisex approach to childrearing. When seriously pursued, the unisex approach results in the crimes of neglecting children's needs and sexual infidelity toward one's spouse. Let's see how
this happened in the case of Karla.

4

A Unisex Parent
in Court

We have seen how the mother's and father's childrearing practices have an important influence on their child's sexual-identity development. The sex-role examples of the parents provide a learning situation for the child. The father's active leadership in the home and his affectionate involvement with his sons and daughters has strong impact on promoting their normal sexual identification. At the same time, the mother's positive attitude toward men and her submission to the father's leadership in the home are important for normal sexual identification in both her sons and daughters.

Temptations for homosexual activity by teen-agers could be substantially reduced if families realized these facts and if they made concerted efforts to provide this kind of healthy home life for children. Much homosexual temptation of teen-agers would be prevented if the parents would live a normal and happy heterosexual married life as an example to their children. When the fathers provide leadership in the home and express manly affection and care for their wives, sons, and daughters, then sexual-identity conflicts in their children are rare. When mothers submit to their husbands' leadership and show womanly affection and care for their husbands, sons, and daughters, then normal sexual identification can result in the children.

The vast majority of parents want their children to grow up with the potential for a normal, heterosexual married life. Parents, by and large, really do hope that their children will grow up to have fulfillment in their own families. And parents usually look forward to happy years when they can have a fulfilling relationship with their grandchildren.

But if all parents knew exactly how to promote future fulfillment for their children, would they devote themselves to the childrearing tasks to do so? Are all parents unselfishly concerned about helping their children to avoid homosexual temptations?

Unfortunately, many parents are more concerned about pursuing their own self-fulfillment and momentary self-gratification than they are about serving their children's welfare. Tragically, this is short-sighted for a parent, because a selfish focus on one's own present desires and wants will undermine the future fulfillment that a parent can enjoy with his or her grandchildren. And failure to serve the best interests of one's child is a shortcut to long-term misery for both the child and the parent.

But some parents are rebellious. They rebel against mutual co-operation and submission in a loving marriage. They rebel against the idea of personal sacrifice for their spouse and children. They rebel against the long-established superiority of normal family life for healthy child development. They rebel against the idea that they may have to set aside their own momentary selfish desires to serve their family's needs first. They rebel against sexual fidelity to their marriage partner. They rebel against the norm of heterosexuality. And in a final sense, they are therefore rebelling against their role and responsibility as a parent.

This kind of rebellion involves a self-deception by the parent. Somehow, the parent comes up with a different way of thinking—rationalizations, if you will—to convince himself or herself that neglect of normal family commitments is all right if one is seeking self-fulfillment in some other way. This was a tragic lesson of *Kramer versus Kramer*.

Instead of examining the plot of this all-too-real movie, let's turn our attention to a case of a parent's self-deception that jeopardized her children's future welfare. Let's see how that mother's confusion led her into captivity to a perverted and selfish pursuit of self-gratification, as opposed to her responsible role as a mother.

This case may be an extreme one to make a point, but I believe it reflects the trends toward sexual confusion, selfish pursuits, and neglect of parental duty so prevalent in contemporary America. Each of us needs to ask, "Where did Karla go wrong? Am I like Karla in any way?"

In the spring of 1979, I was asked to evaluate a family for the purpose of testifying in court as an expert psychological witness. This was a unique court case in which a publicly-admitted bisexual mother was suing her husband for divorce and custody of three preschool-age daughters, who were residing with their father at the time. The mother's case was heavily supported by "gay liberation" and radical feminist groups and individuals who sought to establish a new judicial precedent. These activists hoped that the court would award custody of the children to the parent with an acknowledged homosexual relationship, to establish a new trend in society that would encourage homosexuality.

In court, Karla (as I'll call her) testified that she had previously married as a teen-ager as a means to get out of her parents' home. Karla had casually discarded that first marriage when it became convenient to live on her own. She then joined the Air Force, which she also eventually grew to dislike. Karla therefore revealed her homosexual practices as a means to get a discharge. Later, she married a second time, this time to a man I'll call Frank, who completed his doctorate in a field of psychology. The children were born while Karla was in training as a nurse.

While working as a nurse, Karla developed yet another homosexual relationship, this time with a nurse who worked with her in the obstetrics and gynecology department of a hospital. During the first several months of the youngest daughter's life, Karla left her husband to move into the home of Lois, her homosexual lover. At the same time, Karla led her husband to believe that she wanted to move the family from Georgia to Maine to be near her own parents' home.

Frank therefore resigned his position as a psychologist with a state agency and moved with the two older daughters to the vicinity of his in-laws. Karla later arrived in Maine with the youngest daughter, but subsequently moved back to Georgia to live with Lois. It was then that Karla decided to file for divorce and to sue for the custody of her three children. Karla received heavy gay liberation and feminist backing for her case.

My evaluation of Karla included interviewing, which was tape-recorded. What follows is an abridged portion of the interview, with my comments in the right-hand column to highlight some significant points in the interview. Although this case, including the entire transcribed interview, is a matter of public record in the state courts, I have changed identifying names and locations to protect the welfare of the children.

Interview	*Commentary*
Doctor Rekers: I thought what I'd do is ask you some questions. I have a little bit of background information here. In front of me here is the report written by the social worker who did the home visit.	
Karla: Um-hum, custody is still his.	
Doctor: Um-hum. I've talked to your husband Frank, so I have some background. . . .	The court had awarded temporary custody of the children to the father until the case could be heard in court.
Karla: Um-hum.	
Doctor: Okay. If I have it right, right now the girls are in Maine with Frank.	
Karla: That's right.	Frank lived in Maine with the three daughters, but Karla chose to move back to Georgia with her homosexual lover. Consequently, Karla saw her daughters for only two weeks in the twelve-month period before the hearing.
Doctor: And when was the last time you saw them?	
Karla: In January this year.	
Doctor: And how long were they down?	
Karla: Two weeks, a little over two.	
Doctor: When you left Frank, had you thought at that time that there was even a remote possibility that you might lose permanent custody of the children?	
Karla: Um- I had thought that ah- there might be a hassle over it. Um- and that's one thing that kept me from leaving him for a long time before I did.	
Doctor: Um-hum. So you had thought about that and finally by the time you had decided to leave Frank, it was worth the risk to you?	
Karla: Um- I think, but when I decided I was just under so much stress at that time I just um- couldn't stand to be with him anymore and I had to leave.	The humanistic, self-centered value system justifies the termination of the marriage contract on selfish grounds. Note how often Karla uses the word *I* here and throughout the interview.
Doctor: I'm trying to piece together the chronology, which is hard to do. When you left Frank, this was about the time when there were plans to move to Maine, right?	
Karla: We had been talking about it.	
Doctor: Okay. So you had thought about	

leaving Frank because things just weren't getting along well, but you hesitated because you thought about the children.

Karla: Well, that's one of the reasons that I think, well, they're [the problems with the marriage] not that bad, I'll just see if I can't work it out and go on and talk myself out of it.

Doctor: By the time you left it was a time of real stress.

Karla: Yah. So many things just happened at once, that I just felt like um-he was not a help to me at all. He was no- no support and um- I was working full-time and he was working, too, full-time and I didn't even get to have my own money and I just felt like if I couldn't even have my own money, he wasn't helping me at all, why- why should I be there, I just didn't see any point in it at all.

Doctor: Okay, then he moved to Maine, right, and—

Karla: We were- well, we were both going to go to Maine and my youngest daughter got really sick so I stayed behind with her. Originally I was going to take all the kids and go and he was going to drive by himself and then Diane got really sick and was in the hospital and so I stayed with her, had nothing really to do with the two older girls, so he said that he would take them to my mother's house out there and then I could come when she got out of the hospital which is what happened.

Doctor: So he drove to Maine with the two little girls and then you came later with the little one. Okay. But then at the time he left with the two older girls, you had already decided to leave him, right?

Karla: Yah, we'd already been separated for ah- I can't, it's hard for me to remember the exact date now 'cause it's been so long but we separated in March and we left- he left in, oh, I think it was like the first week of May.

Doctor: Okay, So you were thinking of moving to Maine but not living with him.

Note the self-centered rather than a family-centered attitude.

Notice how self-centered Karla is. She does not see any "point in it at all" when she describes her family situation. Her children's welfare or her husband's welfare are not her concern. This is an exaggeration to state Frank was not helping "at all." Actually, he was a devoted father and hard-working husband.

On such important matters as the breakup of the family and the interstate move of her daughters, Karla cannot remember the time sequence very well—revealing her lack of deep concern for the family unit.

Karla: See we were all good friends at the time. We were on really friendly terms.

Doctor: So you wanted to be in Maine to be with the girls . . . , not for him. Of course, you have relatives.

Karla: My family's there and um- one of the reasons that I had decided to go out there at all, I had- I had two main reasons. One reason- this is complicated. When we split up, we decided that we would stay in Atlanta and then that we would go ahead and sell that house so that we could split the money from the house and everything and we would stay here. My mother called me hysterically one morning, she'd been having a lot of trouble with my father and wanted me to come—I'm the oldest—to come and help her out. She was really having a hard time.

Doctor: So she was up in the air.

Karla: Yah, and she's got two kids at home.

Doctor: And- and Frank wanted to move there at that point.

Karla: Yah.

Doctor: So, okay. So you went up there after the little one was well enough to take her, and then how long did you stay?

Karla: Briefly. I think they added it up to thirteen days.

Doctor: Thirteen days?

Karla: Thirteen days, something like that, altogether.

Doctor: Why did you come back? Then you came back to Atlanta, right?

Karla: Um-hum.

Doctor: Why did you come back?

Karla: Um- Frank called. [Karla cleared her throat.] When I got there he ah- I had asked him if he would go to his cousin's in Vermont when I got to my mother's house. He was also staying at Mother's house. So that I could be with my family and with the kids since I hadn't seen them in a couple of weeks and all of us get together and then I would rent a place and he could come back and this would be a lot more comfortable that way than everybody milling around

In a few paragraphs, it will be apparent that "friendly" does not exactly describe Karla's attitude.

The difficulties in maintaining stable marriages appear to be evidenced elsewhere in Karla's family.

Earlier in this interview, Karla claimed that she and Frank were on "really friendly terms" but here she said she wanted him out of Maine when she arrived at her parents' house.

together. I got to Maine and stayed with my mother for a week or something like that. Frank called, "Could he visit the children for the weekend?" That's what he wanted to know and I said yes he could- he said he picked them up at my mother's- I think it was a Wednesday afternoon and he wanted to keep them until Saturday or Sunday or something like that- May 30 anyway. . . . But he left me a note saying that I wouldn't see the kids until the custody issue was settled and just this long nasty letter to me. And ah- if I wanted to contact him I could write his mother- I think that's what he said. So I just fell apart. I didn't know what to do- um I didn't know where he'd gone. I knew a couple of possibilities and then I thought they were too obvious like Vermont, and his brother was in Connecticut and a few places like that. Then I thought, he's probably gone back to Atlanta and I called up a few friends and they said yes, they had talked to him and thought he was on his way back to Atlanta, and I talked to this friend that said he ah- that's an attorney and he said ah- in most states you can't file for custody of your children unless they're in possession but in Georgia you can. He said I think you should file the divorce papers right away no matter what- and he told me- thought several people told me this- that I should come back so ah-

Doctor: So that's when you initiated court proceedings in Georgia for dissolution of the marriage and custody.

Karla: Um-hum.

Doctor: If you had custody of the children would you be working full-time or part-time or not at all?

Karla: I'd be working.

Doctor: Full-time or part-time?

Karla: . . . I would have to wait and see. . . .

Doctor: Okay. Now since the children have been in Maine, have you made attempts to see them?

Karla: In January. And I talk to them on the

Note that Karla abandoned her husband and three daughters for a homosexual relationship with Lois. Now, as she recalls Frank's attempts to preserve what is left of a normal family life, Karla focuses on describing her own feelings, rather than showing concern for her preschool daughters' welfare.

Note that Karla is not committed to a full-time mothering role for her preschool-age children. Before her separation she worked full-time outside of the home, even though her three daughters were all under four years of age and her husband was employed as a full-time psychologist with an adequate salary.

phone really as frequently as I could. I write them letters and send them things. And I haven't been able to go out there because I just haven't had the money. I had to make a choice between um- it's really been a hard choice to make but I really felt like if I spent all my money like going back to see them and back here and all and I couldn't pay attorneys and I would never get them. And I'd never have them to raise them. And so I had to kind of not see them as often as I'd like to in order to be able to have them all the time.

Doctor: Did you think of living with them in Maine?

Karla: Yah, and I will if I lose. I'm going to go up there, wherever he's going to live.

Doctor: What made you decide not to live in Maine for the time being?

Karla: Right now?

Doctor: Yah.

Karla: I didn't have a cent. There's no way I could have even made it back to Maine. When I first left and then I thought, I want my kids out of this. That's the whole thing, they're the most important thing in the world for me and I just feel like where I'm at now is, and then Georgia with the people that are here to testify for me and everything, it's the way to get them.

Doctor: You didn't think of, say, living with your mother up there? To be with them?

Karla: Um-hum [no].

Doctor: What role did your friend Lois play in your deciding to come back to Georgia rather than being in Maine near your children?

Karla: She didn't play any role. She didn't want to come back to Georgia. She didn't. She didn't want to.

Doctor: Did she have a job back here?

Karla: Um.

Doctor: She was unemployed.

Karla: Oh, you mean before she left?

Doctor: Um-hum.

Karla: Yah, oh yah.

Even though all three daughters are preschool age, and the youngest was (at the time) only a few months old, Karla chose to live in Georgia with Lois, rather than to arrange to live near her children in Maine. This was the fact of her actions, although Karla found it difficult to admit in those terms.

This is an evasion of the truth, because Karla and Frank had divided the equity from the house they sold, and Karla could have stayed with relatives in Maine once she had arrived there. She didn't need to spend the money she spent flying back to Georgia to be with Lois. She could have stayed in Maine with her mother, who invited her, and she could have initiated legal proceedings in Maine.

Lois had accompanied Karla to Maine, but needed to return to her job in Georgia.

"Unemployed" was a half-truth, referring to Lois not having a job in Maine. I didn't drop the question but pursued the full truth.

Doctor: She had a job?
Karla: Um-hum.
Doctor: She had a job back in Georgia?
Karla: Um-hum [yes].
Doctor: Did you look for a job when you were in Maine?
Karla: Many.
Doctor: And you were there thirteen days, right?
Karla: Um-hum.
Doctor: Did you consider filing for custody in Maine?
Karla: I didn't think I could.
Doctor: Well, obviously you can file for custody any place.
Karla: Not if you don't have your children. Not if I've been ripped off.
Doctor: Did you check with attorneys in Maine . . . ?
Karla: Um-hum [no]. I just checked with this friend in Georgia.
Doctor: Do you live with Lois now?
Karla: Uh-huh.
Doctor: In a house?
Karla: Uh-huh.
Doctor: Okay, according to this report, you had chosen to live in a homosexual relationship but now you're saying you've decided not to if you get custody—
Karla: That's right.
Doctor: If you don't get custody you're going to continue?
Karla: Probably.
Doctor: And according to the report, you would explain to your girls what homosexual relationships are?
Karla: Yes, if they asked.
Doctor: If they asked about it? You would tell them that you've been involved in homosexual relationships?
Karla: If they asked.
Doctor: If they asked you about it. Okay, the way I said it, would you want to raise your girls in such a way that they could successfully take on the role of the mother and the wife and be satisfied with that role in the

Lois was employed in Georgia, which made it problematic for Karla to live with Lois but be close to her daughters as well. Karla chose to live with her lover in Georgia rather than be near her preschool-age children.

In the four-month period between the time the social worker interviewed Karla and the time of this interview, Karla demonstrated her instability and lack of long-term commitments to people by deciding not to live with Lois if she were given custody. Note the word *probably*, indicating no long-term commitment to a sexual relationship.

Note that Karla offers no age guidelines as to when she would tell her girls about her deviant sex life. She says only that she would tell them "if they asked."

future? Would you want them to have the
capacity to develop that kind of role?

Karla: Yes, I want them to could be able to,
but I wouldn't want to limit them.

Doctor: So you wouldn't. What if they grew
up to have an interest in a homosexual relationship? That would interfere with the
capacity to be totally satisfied with just being
a wife and mother.

Karla: Well, I- I don't know that most women
are totally satisfied with being a wife and
mother anyway. I—

Doctor: I mean just successfully satisfy themselves that they can live with a husband and
be a mother. Do you want your girls to live
with that capacity?

Karla: Um, I would prefer that they would be
heterosexual.

Doctor: Why would you prefer that?

Karla: Because it's easier for them.

Doctor: Because it's easier for them or for
you?

Karla: Both.

Doctor: Do you think that you have an influence on your girls' development to become
heterosexual or homosexual?

Karla: Um- I suppose I must have some influence. How much I don't know. I just-I really
don't know. I mean there's so many different
areas of thought in that I just don't know
what one I believe or if I believe any of it.

Doctor: Well then, do you think, say, the example or model of your life would have any
influence if they observe how you live—do
you think that makes a difference in them?

Karla: Yah, I think it does. But I'm saying
how much—really in the long run I don't
know. I mean some people say it's biological
and people are saying this that and the other.
And then their friends have so much influence after they go to school and their peer
group and parents of their friends and all
that too, um—

Doctor: Well, if—if your preference is that
they grow up to be heterosexual, how could
you use whatever influence you have? If

Karla does not value heterosexual marriage as the desired
norm for herself or for her
daughters.

Karla tries to rationalize her
viewpoint by supposing that
most women are not satisfied
with being a wife and mother.

Notice that the basic value
Karla reveals is pragmatism.
She prefers heterosexuality for
her daughters because it is
"easier," not because it is right.

Karla is very uncomfortable
with thinking about her influence on her daughters.

Karla tries to rationalize away
her influence by example upon
her children.

you have custody of the children you would be the primary parent. How would you use the influence that you do have to influence them to become heterosexual, given that the model example of your life is completely different from that?

Karla: How is the model and the example of my life completely different if I'm not active in homosexuality?

Doctor: Well, you're not living with the father.

Karla: Well, neither are most of the women in my age group, that I know. I mean many, many women are divorced and raising children. That's sort of becoming the norm nowadays.

Doctor: My question though was, how would you influence them . . . ?

Karla: How would I influence them to be heterosexual, is that what you're saying?

Doctor: Given the easiest way to do that is to be living with their father. . . .

Karla: Given that I'm a single mother and they not having a male around the house.

Doctor: See, you're not doing it the conventional way, so how are you going to do it?

Karla: First of all, they're completely exposed to heterosexuality through television, books, school. Um- our society is heterosexual. That's what they see.

Doctor: Is that all they see?

Karla: No, that's not all they see. I think that's the overwhelming impact. Just television even. And ah—

Doctor: But if you were the closest person to them—

Karla: Well, most of my friends are heterosexual. I have a lot of married couple friends . . . and those are the people that I see. People from work and all mostly with little kids.

Doctor: You- you'd also be seeing Lois?

Karla: Well, most people have single friends too.

Doctor: And what if they asked you about having a homosexual relationship, you would tell them?

Karla: Uh-huh. Sure would.

Here Karla pretends that she will cease all homosexual activity when rearing her daughters, but in other places she boldly states a plan to reveal her homosexuality to her daughters.
Notice that Karla cites the average behavior as a norm. If most people lie, does that make lying a norm?

"Completely"? What about homosexuals visible on TV, in magazines, school, and society? If the girls' mother tells them she is homosexual, the daughters might notice and imitate other homosexuals on TV and in society all the more.

At this point in the interview, notice how certain Karla is that she will tell her daughters about her homosexual relationships.

Doctor: If they asked you about Lois, if she was the one, would you tell them?

Karla: Uh-huh. Yah. How much I would tell them when, I think depends on what age they are and how they're doing. I'm not saying if Mary, who's not three yet, comes up, and not that she could ask something like that, but if she did I wouldn't tell her, I don't think. But as they get older I think I would just use my judgment as to how much information they could take.

Doctor: But you're saying that there's nothing that you could do—

Karla: Also, they have a father. You know, they have a father and they can be with their father and—

Doctor: But if you're in Georgia, they're not going to be with him much. It'll be the reverse of—

Karla: If he's not- if he doesn't come back to Georgia. I'll be surprised if he doesn't come back.

Doctor: Okay, so you're saying that there's nothing much you could do to influence personally their heterosexual development. It's more other moms they see in society, TV, or see their friends....

Karla: I think you bring ah- but I'm the catalyst for all that, too. Bringing the friends around, taking them to friends' houses, really choosing who they're going to see when they're small—

Doctor: So you're saying—

Karla: Um- so I do see myself being in control of that.

Doctor: But you'll try to teach them by saying: hear what I say, don't do what I do.

Karla: No. I just think it's that they'll- that's what they'll be exposed to and I really think that's probably what they become. But um- I'm not going to try to say that if they- if they ask me about it or anything. I would just explain to them that I think it's easier to be a heterosexual and hopefully they can be happy that way. If they can be happy that way, more power to them. They're better off.

The father presently lives in Maine and the mother lives in Georgia.

Karla finds herself making the inconsistent point that she would tell her daughters that she is a homosexual but at the same time she prefers (so she said) that her daughters grow up as heterosexuals. But she is not sure how she could accomplish that goal, given her own deviant example to the girls.

And if they can't then they should think
about it. Discuss it with people.

Doctor: So you're going to take the approach
that they can decide on their own which
they prefer—

Karla: Of course, they can decide. Everybody
does but ah—

Doctor: At what age will they decide?

Karla: I don't know. I have no idea.

Doctor: Do you think that you decided?

Karla: Um- I suppose you'd call it a decision.
I think it's something I always knew sort of
way in the back of my mind but really
ignored for a long, long time. And finally
what I decided to do was face it. So I guess I
did.

Doctor: So, what was your decision then?

Karla: To really realize that I was a bisexual
person and ah- that's the way I was.

Doctor: You're not satisfied with just a sexual
relationship with a man?

Karla: It depends on the man.

Doctor: By "bisexual" do you mean—sexual
relationships with both men and women?

Karla: Um-hum [yes].

Doctor: So you wouldn't be satisfied with
just one or the other?

Karla: I might be. I'm saying I could have
sexual relationships with a man or a woman.

Doctor: So you're not quite sure which you
prefer.

Karla: I think in different times of my life, I've
preferred men and different times women.

Doctor: Um-hum.

Karla: But I'm really not willing to put a label
on myself saying this is the way that I'm
going to be for the rest of my life. I am a lesbian and that's it for the next fifty years.
Period. I'm never going to go to bed with
another man, I'm never going to be involved
with another man, or likewise that I'm a
heterosexual. I just don't feel comfortable
doing that right now.

Doctor: You don't have the capacity to make
a permanent sexual commitment to one
person?

Note that Karla states a belief in
choosing one's own sexual
behavior.

Here Karla's language suggests
her own choice, as well as an
awareness of being one of
those people tempted by homosexual desires.

Note the completely autonomous basis for ethical decisionmaking that Karla reveals. She
reveals no basis for sexual
ethics except what she autono-
mously prefers to do.

Karla does not expect herself to
make lifetime sexual
commitments.

Notice that Karla's basis for
sexual ethics is her own feelings of the moment.

Karla: I think I do.

Doctor: You just said that you didn't think you could.

Karla: I have learned from the last year to never say never.

Doctor: So you don't have the capacity?

Karla: What do you mean?

Doctor: From what you've learned in life, you'd never feel that you can make a sexual relation of commitment to just one person.

Karla: I feel that anything is possible.

Doctor: In the future. But what you're saying is that you've learned in the past year that you can't count on any one relationship.

Karla: No. I'm not saying that at all. I'm saying that things are not at all what I expected my life to be so ah- I'm just saying I'm leaving myself open to possibilities.

Doctor: Would you want your girls to develop a capacity to make a single commitment to a sexual relationship with one person for a lifetime?

Karla: Um-hum. If they were happy that way. I want them to be what they're going to be and to be happy, with constructive lives, be self-reliant and um-um I don't want life to be hard on them. So I want them to be the things that are easiest for them to be and to be able to get along and fit into society. But um, if they're not that way, then they're not. You know, I really think they will be but ah—

Doctor: What- how much influence would you have?

Karla: How much influence would I have- we've already discussed that.

Doctor: You're not sure how much.

Karla: No, I'm really not. I'm not sure who's got the most influence or what or whether it's innate—do you see—what I'm saying. I'm just not positive about it. I think that the family has quite a bit of influence but. . . .

Doctor: What would be the biggest influence? One single biggest influence.

Karla: When- when I- I don't know, when I looked at myself, I feel like I've always been my own biggest influence. When I try to

Note Karla's illogical doubletalk, which is a result of her relativistic, humanistic views.

Note that Karla does not expect herself to make a commitment to a sexual relationship with just one person. This value system produces a self-fulfilling prophecy.

The humanistic ideal of "openness" is Karla's creed. This is another way of saying "lack of fidelity or commitment."

Notice that Karla's basic value is self-centered *happiness* of the individual. This is materialistic humanism and pragmatism, with no ethical norm recognized outside of self-gratification. Karla acknowledges the reality that homosexual pursuits result in trouble with living in society. She knows from personal experience how her homosexual choices have disrupted her own, her husbands', and her daughters' lives.

Here Karla acknowledges the importance of the child's family for sexual adjustment.

Here Karla recognizes that she determines her own behavior by choices, and that her behav-

think was it my mother or father, or particular teachers or friends or anything, um- well I guess it probably was like my mother but I just took certain things from them and developed certain ideas and just-you know that was my ah- basis for making decisions. And I guess it was probably from my parents, even though I seem to be different from them and my ideas are different. Basically what I, how I learned to be that way was from things that they said. Do you see what I mean?

Doctor: That was—

Karla: So I guess that the parents probably are. I mean like, my parents taught me to be honest, you know, you don't steal things from other people, you're a patriotic citizen and all this, and their method of doing it and my method of doing that are two different things but we're still both that way.

Doctor: Okay, well, what um- what kind of standard then have you picked up for what's right or what's honest or what's wrong?

Karla: I can't answer a big broad question like that. Just be more specific and I could answer it.

Doctor: ... how would you teach your children how to tell whether something's right or wrong?

Karla: In terms of what? Give me an example. I have a very hard time answering real broad questions. If you'll be more specific I'll answer it.

Doctor: Well, do you have a childrearing philosophy—a way of going about raising children? What strategy would you have to go about teaching them right and wrong?

Karla: That's the same question. Can you give me like a specific example for little kids and I'll tell you what I would do?

Doctor: Well, no. That's your job, I'm asking you to answer that. Raising children is a whole bunch of specifics, but you have some approach to teaching all of the specifics. Some consistent approach?

Karla: Um-hum.

ior is not totally determined by environmental factors.

Karla brings up the issues of ethics and morality, so I ask her for her own basis for right and wrong.

In this very revealing answer, Karla acknowledges that she has no ethical standard for determining right and wrong, outside of her own arbitrary feelings regarding each specific ethical decision.

Karla is at a loss to provide any general ethical basis for deciding right from wrong. It is no wonder, therefore, that she has no sexual ethic beyond her own feelings.

Doctor: I'm asking you how would you teach them how to know what's right and what's wrong in terms of decisions they have to make for themselves.

Karla: What types of decisions? I just- I can't answer that and I can sit and think about it and something will come, but right now nothing is coming.

Doctor: Okay, how about honesty? What is honesty?

Karla: Um-hum. I think they should always be honest unless it's some harmless little ah- say like um- hurting, you know, your grandmother's feelings with her ugly hat rather than that's a horrible hat, you should take it back to the store you know. They could say, you know, 'what a nice hat you got.' Um- I think in ah- big things you should be honest, you should try to be honest with your feelings to yourself and other people as much as you can. Ah- I don't think that you should cheat on your income tax or anything like that. I think you should be honest in that way and I suppose you start teaching them by you know if they find a dime on the floor give it back to the person that dropped it type- type thing. You know, start with that.

Doctor: What would you teach the girls about marriage? As they grow up?

Karla: Sometimes a man and woman want to live together and for the rest of their lives and when they decide that, they meet each other and fall in love and they do what's called getting married. It's a little ceremony that people go through and they get a piece of paper saying that they can live together. And sometimes people live together for the rest of their lives and sometimes they decide that they don't want to live together anymore and they do what's called getting a divorce. When they're married they usually have children and they live in the same house and work and they do things together as a family.

Doctor: Okay, would you teach them that's a better arrangement than other arrangements?

Karla: No.

Karla has no knowledge of general ethical norms to teach children, to guide them in their encounters with decisions regarding right and wrong. She does not even mention simple norms, such as respecting other people's rights and property.

For someone like Karla who has twice married and promised sexual fidelity "till death do us part," I thought it would be important to find out how she defined honesty in terms of a standard of right and wrong.

Karla confuses brutal opinion-stating (the example of the ugly hat) with honesty and begins her definition of honesty with this type of situational-ethic exception.

Karla's norm is to be honest "as much as you can"—not a very demanding norm—then excuse her dishonesty by pleading to herself that greater honesty was too hard to achieve.

Karla's basis for marriage is "falling in love," and includes the concept of easy divorce if she later feels differently. She makes no mention of moral commitment. Notice that the ethics of marriage to Karla depend on the partner's romantic feelings over time and not upon a commitment of love and caring. This teaching will not result in stable, long-term, happy, and fulfilling marriages.

Doctor: Or it's just an optional—

Karla: I think it's an option. Nowadays especially as the way things are really opening up.

Doctor: Um-hum. Now, did you make the divorce decision when you left Frank? You said that you were under a lot of stress then but, of course, if you're under a lot of stress in one particular time period, you could take time to rethink a long-range decision.

Karla: Um-hum.

Doctor: Filing for divorce is a long-term decision compared to walking out of the house one day.

Karla: Um-hum. When I filed for divorce, he had stolen my children. I was absolutely enraged and there was no way that I would ever-ever go back with him after that. Anybody that would do something like that to another person, just in my book—

Doctor: You could never forgive him?

Karla: Well- I think I'm coming close now and able to- I'm not angry at him anymore like I was but no, I could never trust him anymore, the way that I used to, never.

Doctor: So you decided you could never live with him even though that was the only way to get close to the children?

Karla: No, I've tried to, I've talked to him even though I didn't want to live with him but that if I could be near the children I would come back and live with him in the house but he didn't want to.

Doctor: Under the current court order that he has temporary custody, does that allow you to visit the children?

Karla: I have to get some kind of- there's no provisions for visitation.

Doctor: How did you get visitation in January?

Karla: I have to- I went to court. I went to court and got it.

Doctor: So you could go to court and get visitation rights.

Karla: Uh-huh.

Karla has consciously or unconsciously accepted the rhetoric of humanism that teaches that stable marriage is no more preferred than divorce or homosexuality. This short-sighted humanistic world view ignores the welfare of the spouse and children, sacrificing them on the altar of *self*-gratification.

Within the humanistic value system, there is no logical basis for trusting another person. Trust is reduced to a mere irrational feeling.

Note that Frank did not take custody of the children until *after* Karla had moved out of his home to live with Lois. *After* Frank took loving custody of his daughters to protect them from their mother's unstable and illegal sexual lifestyle, Karla uses this protective action by Frank as her excuse for filing for divorce. Notice that her rationalization for filing for divorce is again based on her *feelings* only—her anger at Frank for taking the daughters into his protective care.

Doctor: If you were in Maine you could go to court and be visiting your children.

Karla: Um-hum.

Doctor: Are you going?

Karla: Well, no, I think you have to go to court down here. Well, maybe not.

Doctor: But you haven't made any other arrangements to be with them other than that period of time?

Karla: They're two thousand miles away. I don't have- you know, I don't have time off from work to be able- if I quit my job I wouldn't have any money.

Doctor: How about getting a job in Maine?

Karla: Then I would lose the case because I wouldn't be down. I wouldn't be a resident in Georgia. And I wouldn't have any ah-claim. And this is where the people are that know me. If I go to Maine and fight this case, nobody knows me out there. You know, I don't have a pediatrician I've been going to for years and a babysitter and all that stuff who know who I am.

Doctor: Well, you have your mother and sisters in Maine.

Karla: Well, yeah, but that's a relative and they'll go and say aren't you her mother— that's not that great of a witness in terms of court and all.

Doctor: A witness to establish what? To establish your character?

Karla: Um-hum.

Doctor: Have you told your girls anything about lesbians or lesbianism so far?

Karla: No.

Doctor: How do you show affection to the children?

Karla: I hug them and kiss them and tell them I love them and call them nicknames.

Doctor: Anything else?

Karla: Those are the main things.

Doctor: Do you count things like dressing them, or feeding them, or giving them baths and things like that?

Karla: Well, they really dress themselves mostly, except the baby. I count ah-dressing

Karla's concern for being with her children is so weak that in twelve months of separation from them, she has not checked into the legal process of how she could obtain more visitation rights during the interim period until the hearing.

Remember that Karla and Frank had divided the equity from the sale of their house.

Actually, Karla neglects to add that her homosexual lover resides in Georiga with her and the homosexual activists supporting her case also reside in the South.

Once again, love or affection to Karla is just a feeling or a communication of a feeling. Her understanding of love does not also include a trustworthy commitment to be always depended upon for providing care.

and feeding and bathing as much more learning experiences for the kids.

Doctor: Do you have a philosophy of disciplining your children?

Karla: I believe in being consistent.

Doctor: Consistent?

Karla: Um-hum.

Doctor: Um- could you give me an example of being consistent?

Karla: Well, if I tell one of the children to do something then they're going to do it. If it's- or if they've done something wrong, and I say go to your room, and they say no, they're going to go to their room, that's all there is to it. And then the next time they do that they're also going to go to their room. Um- that type of thing.

Doctor: Did you send any child support to Frank?

Karla: I sent clothes and toys and things to the kids and I'm not sending him money.

Doctor: Um-hum. Why not—why don't you send him money? Has he taken care of their needs, since he's had them, all their needs?

Karla: I don't know. I doubt it. I think that just things- it's all hearsay so it's hard for me to tell you.

Doctor: Is there any way that you've tried to fill in the gap if you doubt that he's supplying their needs? Have you made any attempt to fulfill them yourself?

Karla: I just talk to the kids. That's about all I can do is talk to them.

Doctor: And when you talk to them, what impression do you get- do you get the impression that their needs are filled or not?

Karla: Well, they cry and scream and tell me they want to come home to Georgia so you know, I doubt it.

Doctor: Do you try to think of any ways to solve that problem at the moment?

Karla: Getting custody of the kids is my solution of it. You know, obviously it seems like you really disagree about it, but that's my decision and that's the way that I feel is the right thing to do and the right way to go.

Even though Karla says she doubts that Frank was adequately caring for her daughters, and even though Frank was unemployed while Karla herself was employed, she did not send Frank any financial support for the daughters.

Karla's only interpretation of her daughters' distress is that they want to be with her instead of with their father. Actually, the little girls wanted both parents.

Note Karla's basis for right and wrong. She "feels" that divorcing her husband and suing for custody of the girls is the right thing to do when she was tempted to be sexually unfaithful to her husband and left him to live with a lesbian.

Doctor: I'm just asking questions.

Karla: Well, I know, but you keep harping on that so.

Doctor: I'm trying to find out to what extent are you weighing the children's needs against your own desires to be with Lois. Which is more important to you? To be with Lois or with the kids?

Karla: You've obviously been talking to Frank.

Doctor: I'm asking you, I'm not asking him.

Karla: It's much more important to be with the kids. Lois and I really don't have a sexual relationship anymore. We're really friends. Um- in a way this whole thing is really kind of- kind of ridiculous.
Um- we're not going to live together anymore and so obviously it's more, *much more* important to me to get the kids. She knows that. She's always known it. And she's not real, real thrilled about, you know, having to move out, it's going to be much more expensive. But I've just said, I'm sorry there's nothing I can do. The kids are first and you're not and never will be.

Notice the quality of the homosexual relationship between Karla and Lois. It is not a stable relationship. Of course, this is difficult to determine because Karla is in the self-serving process of making herself appear qualified to gain child custody. It is, therefore, uncertain here what her true feelings are. She was told that she had a better chance to win her case if she moved out of the house with her homosexual lover.

Doctor: Okay. In childrearing, would you raise a girl differently than a boy?

Karla: I would hope that I wouldn't. But I think that subtly I would.

Doctor: In what ways would it be different?

Karla: Um- I would just ah- like I have a girl friend who has a boy and a girl and she has really tried not to raise them differently- but just things like her nickname for the boy was much more rough and tumbling and the sweet little nickname for the girl and things that she'd really done subconsciously and she looked back two or three years later and realized what she had done. That's what ... that type of thing.

Notice that Karla has accepted the radical feminist doctrine that boys and girls are to be reared identically, as if there were no differences between them.

Doctor: Why would you hope that you wouldn't treat a girl different than a boy?

Karla: I think that we have certain basic human values that need to be brought across to a member of either sex and that the sexes were ah- became closer together instead of being so far apart and certain things are

By "basic human values," Karla is referring to humanistic values.

acceptable for men and certain things are acceptable for women, we'd have a much better society. And you have to start with the children, that's ah- then they have to grow up with these human values.

Doctor: The only way people can get along better is to be identical, the same?

Karla: I don't think they have to be the same. But I mean um- okay like it being unacceptable for men to cry, things like that. I don't think that that should be unacceptable. You know, I think- it should be acceptable for everybody to cry if they're happy or sad. It's this type of thing.

Doctor: Um-hum. Right.

Karla: It's not being identical, it's being able to be free with your feelings or whatever you want- call it.

Doctor: There are a lot of arbitrary differences like that. It is arbitrary that men can't cry. It's an arbitrary social rule that's destructive. But are there any essential differences between how you should raise a girl and a boy? Given that there are more arbitrary ones than there are essential, but are there any essential ways that you'd raise a girl differently than a boy?

Karla: No, I don't think there are. I think you should raise them the same. I mean like- unless I'm not getting your point. I don't see that you would treat a little boy any different. You would just- I mean like I hug and kiss my little girls and um, you know, do nice things for them and I think you would teach the little boy the same thing now. If you're talking about when they get a little older and they're learning to cook and you know, learning all that stuff- um maybe you would take the kid outside and teach him how to mow the lawn and you know, all that. But I'm going to teach my- daughters are going to learn how to mow the lawn as much as they're going to cook and do the dishes and sew and all that.

Doctor: Um-hum.

Karla: Many boys don't get married so young

Apparently Karla is unhappy that society accepts a woman's faithful sexual relationship with her husband, but does not accept her promiscuous sexual liaisons with other women. She believes society would be "much better" if it allowed a mother like her to have sex with women (as a man is allowed sex with a wife).

Karla would not teach her daughters that sexual relations with a woman are a unique privilege of a man married to her. First, she does not believe that marriage is to be preferred over promiscuity. Second, she hopes to teach boys and girls that there are no differences in what is acceptable for them when they grow up.

Karla insists on focusing on *arbitrary* role differences between males and females in in our society, but she cannot think of any *essential* role differences. She does not show an awareness that girls need to be helped to develop a female sexual identity, including expectations of marrying a man (not having a relationship with a woman) and perhaps becoming a mother.

anymore and they need to know how to do
these things in order to take care of
themselves.

Doctor: Um-hum. Um—

Karla: You obviously dress them differently.

Doctor: What is your policy at home, in
terms of you or other adults appearing without clothes in front of the girls?

Distinctive styles of clothing are
the only differences Karla can
distinguish between boys and
girls.

Karla: [laughing] We don't have a written
policy on that. If it happens, it happens. And
ah- we don't go flashing through the house
but we don't make a big deal about it if anybody sees each other naked. But I do take
baths with them and things like that.

Doctor: Um-hum. Does your philosophy
differ depending on the age of the girls?

Karla: No.

Doctor: No? How would it be different with a
boy?

Karla: This is how I was brought up and I'm
sure that has a lot to do with it-my parents
were real lax about being nude. I suppose
I've grown up with a certain sense of immod-
esty and I think that- but I really think it is a
positive thing.

Karla has no standards about
personal modesty in front of
boys. But it is psychologically
important for mothers to show
modesty in front of boys in
order to reinforce their distinctive male identity. And, by the
same token, fathers should be
more modest in front of daughters than sons, in order to
respect and promote the
daughters' feminine identity.

Doctor: What are the most important things
for you in life in the future? What are your
most important goals for yourself?

Karla: Right now, to be with the kids and to
raise my children. This is the most important
thing.

Doctor: What would be your second after
that?

Karla: Um- I suppose my career. I'd like to go
back to school sometime.

Doctor: Um-hum.

Karla: But mainly I see it as a family-type
thing in being with them. It's very, very
important.

Doctor: Do you value the role of being a
mother?

Karla: Ohhh, yes. Very much.

Doctor: Is the role of being a mother different to you than Frank's role of being a father
to the girls? Is there a difference?

Karla: The difference is I had them.

Doctor: You mean you gave birth to them?

Karla: Yup. They- ah- I just think that there's a special bonding between mothers and babies. Especially mothers and little girls. It just isn't there between a father and a daughter. Like Frank says, he cannot relate to little babies and little girls that can't talk. And there's just something special that you just cannot describe. And it's the most special feeling in the whole world. And I think it's really from a mother and baby and it's 'cause I had the baby and she's mine and I'm hers but like let me give you an example— when I saw Susie in January, after not having seen her for so long I was really worried about how she was going to react to me and how I was going to react to her and really afraid she was going to scream for a week and a half and be so unhappy that she was off in this strange person's house. She cried for about ten minutes after I picked her up. Then she grasped me and clung on to me for two or three days. She tried to nurse. She wouldn't go to anybody else. And ... knew exactly who I was. She did. And I mean it's not only me that said it a lot, other people saw it. And it was just incredible and I just have this really special feeling for her that I had been so afraid I wouldn't have.

Doctor: Um-hum.

Karla: And I just think that's present between a mother and a child that just isn't between them.

Doctor: Do you think your daughters would identify with you more than with the father because they're girls?

Karla: Um-hum. How can they help it?

Doctor: Well, if they identify with you and then they ask you about your sexual orientation do you think that they would then identify with that?

Karla: No, not necessarily. I really think by the time they get old enough to even discuss that you know, in detail, you know, they're going to be pretty big.

This is an ironic statement, given the fact that Karla made little serious attempt to be with her youngest daughter during the time Diane was five to seventeen months old.

Doctor: What age would you tell them about that?

Karla: When they ask. But I imagine the first question would be some sort of innocuous little thing that would require a yes or no answer and I don't think that until they really get to be like in high school—junior high or high school that they would really-you know, early teens I would think, get some sort of—

Doctor: You've said earlier that kids may ask a question, but they may not be ready for—

Karla: Well, they may be asking you- you-you're like sitting there thinking oh, when are they going to ask type thing. And as soon as they say anything, you think oh that's it, I have to say something.

Doctor: Um-hum.

Karla: I'm saying if you just relax and that may not be it at all and give them a brief answer. They'll ask again if they really want to know more.

Doctor: But do you think that you as the parent have to keep any developmental age guidelines in mind? Are you just going to answer anything they might ask if they're persistent enough or are you, as the parent, are you going to use some discretion on your sexual life?

Karla: Like- what type of- of- well it might be none of their business depending on how old they were and when they asked. Yah, I see what you mean.

Doctor: Would you wait to a certain maturity level, even if they asked you about homosexuality? Would you wait until a certain maturity level before you discussed it?

Karla: If I thought they were too young, I might say well let's discuss it later and I'll let you know when you're big enough- it's for big people.

Doctor: What's big for you? How would you define that? What's mature enough?

Karla: Um- it's really hard for me to say 'cause they're really so little.

Doctor: Is six years old big enough?

Note again Karla's lack of age guidelines for telling her girls about her own deviant sexuality. I continued to ask her, in different ways, to provide age guidelines, until I finally had to make it obvious what my view is. Then you will note that Karla changes her story to tell me what she thinks I want to hear—all to appear good because I would be testifying in court about her within a few weeks.

Here, Karla is trying to interpret my viewpoint and she changes her story to agree with me.

Karla: Ah- I don't think so. Depending on the question, what- are you talking about sort of sitting down and having a little discussion about it?

Doctor: Um-hum.

Karla: Um- I wouldn't think six years old would be anything. You could say anything beyond like um- most people ah- fall in love with a- you know, if you're a woman you fall in love with a- if you're a man you fall in love with a woman. Some people ah-some women fall in love with other women and some men fall in love with other men and leave it at that. I think that they could deal with something like that, what do you think or am I expecting too much?

Here Karla acknowledges that she would teach her daughters at age six that homosexual relationships are like marital love and equally acceptable.

Doctor: It depends on the mental age, too, not just their chronological age—how bright they are. And would you wait until a certain age before you talk about the sexual part in sexual relationships? What age would you wait to?

Karla: I don't even know if I would. I mean I don't think I would discuss, tell them about my sexual relations.

Doctor: Um-hum.

Karla: I think that's my own business really. And I don't think I'd go into details with my children 'cause that's none of their business. That's an intimate part of my life and they can have an intimate part of their lives when they get old enough to have it.

Notice how Karla contradicts her earlier statements on this issue, now that she is aware that I believe that a parent should consider the maturity level of a child before revealing deviant sexual conduct.

Doctor: Um-hum. What if they never asked you any questions about sex? Would you approach them at some age?

Karla: Eventually I think I would, but I mean they already have so- I don't think that's realistic.

Doctor: You say that you're bisexual? How do you define that?

Karla: I'm saying that I'm bisexual because legally that's the way that they define me. So I sort of feel an obligation to go along with that term. And a bisexual is a peson who has or has had sexual relationships with members of both sexes. And that's true.

Doctor: Would you want your girls to grow up exclusively to be heterosexual?

Karla: Well, I hate to be all the way on one end of any scale like that.

Doctor: Is it easier for a woman to stay with the father of her children if she's heterosexual as opposed to, say, a bisexual?

Karla: Probably, but depending on the relationship. I mean, they may have an open relationship and ah- . . . they're still together.

Note that Karla's use of the term *open relationship* means "open to adultery."

Doctor: Um-hum.

Karla: And so- I don't know I think it would depend on the two people, probably in general if both people were heterosexual it would be easier.

Doctor: Most people expect fidelity, too.

Karla: Yah, I guess for a while anyway.

Note that Karla does not value a commitment to lifelong sexual fidelity.

Doctor: Oh, I have one final question I just remembered to ask you. When you were under stress and left Frank, at that time did you seek any professional help?

Karla: No.

Doctor: And did you seek help later on?

Karla: I talked to Dr. Doe several times. And um- that helped.

5

The Unisex Road
to Family Disintegration

Karla spoke of a growing "openness" in society that implied freedom for her to pursue sexual activities outside her marriage. The traditional norm of heterosexual marriage is formally rejected by the *Humanist Manifesto*[1] and is implicitly rejected by everything that Karla told me in her interview. In humanistic rhetoric, the breaking of wedding vows is rechristened with the terms *openness* or *freedom* to make the failure of commitment sound laudable.

But is there no such thing as sexual abnormality? If the norm of heterosexual marriage is discarded, then what is normal? I contend that the kind of sexual freedom that Karla advocated for herself and for teaching her own young daughters is not really freedom at all— it is a trap. Regardless of the words used to describe her transitory sexual relationships, we cannot be fooled into believing that Karla was more free than are parents who remain faithful to each other.

In fact, Karla's loose sexual conduct led her to a dead-end trap. This trap was captivity to abnormality. It was a trap with no decent way out. Once she had destroyed her second marriage to the father of her daughters, the family unit would never be the same again— regardless of the outcome of the court decision about child custody. Karla was trapped by an abnormal family situation of her own making. And this was the direct consequence of her modern "openness."

---

1. *Humanist Manifesto Two* (Buffalo, NY: Prometheus Books, 1973) states, ". . . neither do we wish to prohibit, by law or social sanction, sexual behavior between consenting adults. The many varieties of sexual exploration should not in themselves be considered 'evil.' Short of harming others or compelling them to do likewise, individuals should be permitted to express their sexual proclivities and pursue their lifestyles as they desire" (p. 18).

The three little daughters, too, were captive to an abnormal family life for the rest of their lives. They would never again enjoy the happiness of growing up with both biological parents under one roof. The abnormality of their mother trapped the daughters in a childhood of significant separation from one of their parents.

The case of Karla raises several questions. The most immediate ones are, "What did the judge decide? Who was awarded custody of the children—the bisexual mother or the heterosexual father?"

After I quote from the judge's final decisions on custody, I will return to the question, "What is sexual abnormality?" To answer this question, I will have to define what the sexual norm is—something that Karla could not (or would not) do. This, then, will provide the basis for defining homosexuality and for defining sexual-identity disturbances in children. These definitions will clarify who are the captives among us.

Considerations in Karla's Case

Reflecting the Judeo-Christian moral consensus, the law in Karla's state prohibits marriage between two individuals "... unless one party is a male and the other party is a female" (Chapter 741.04). Statute 63.042(3) of the state code further specifies that "no person eligible to adopt under this statute may adopt if that person is a homosexual." Therefore, Karla could not marry Lois, and Lois could not adopt Karla's children as her own by claiming to be a second parent living with Karla.

The Law about Custody

In the state law, Statute 61.13(3), regarding the dissolution of marriage, certain conditions are specified for the judge to consider:

> For purpose of custody, the best interests of the child shall be determined by the court's consideration and evaluation of all factors affecting the best welfare and interests of the child, including, but not limited to:
>
> (a) The love, affection, and other emotional ties existing between the parents and the child.
> (b) The capacity and disposition of the parents to give the child love, affection, and guidance and to continue the educating of the child.

(c) The capacity and disposition of the parents to provide the child with food, clothing, medical care or other remedial care recognized and permitted under the laws of this state in lieu of medical care, and other material needs.

(d) The length of time the child has lived in a stable, satisfactory environment and the desirability of maintaining continuity.

(e) The permanence, as a family unit, of the existing or proposed custodial home.

(f) The *moral fitness of the parents* [italics mine].

(g) The *mental and physical health of the parents* [italics mine].

(h) The home, school, and community record of the child.

(i) The reasonable preference of the child, if the court deems the child to be of sufficient intelligence, understanding, and experience to express a preference.

(j) Any other factor considered by the court to be relevant to a particular child custody dispute.

My evaluation of this family is too extensive to present here. But I recommended to the court, as an expert psychological witness, that custody of the three daughters be awarded to the father, not to the mother.

The Judge's Verdict

The best way to understand the outcome of this court case is to quote portions from the judge's decision regarding the awarding of custody of the three young girls.

[Karla] and [Frank] were married in 1973. Their union produced three daughters, present ages approximately four-and-one-half, two-and-one-half, and one-and-one-half years of age. On March the 3rd, 1978, [Karla] announced to [Frank] that she was gay and was leaving him to pursue a gay life. The youngest child, [Diane], was then some two months old. . . .

. . . there was much psychiatric and psychological testimony in this case, both from a child psychiatrist and three psychologists. Ironically, [Frank] is also a psychologist and was employed as such. . . . Two of his witnesses . . . were either psychologists as well or professionals in the teaching and counselling fields. One thing that becomes very clear in listening to all the testimony on balances, the experts are not in agreement concerning [Karla's] ability to parent these children. Some offer the statement that she was not fit in the sense of capable of parenting these children for various personality reasons in addition to her announced sexual preferences.... But much of the evidence he [Frank] did adduce would tend to indicate that she is a cold and withdrawn person who is unwilling or unable to give the affection small children need. ... The psychological testimony also went to the point of whether as a role model a mother who was a homosexual practicing her homosexual preference can adequately nurture and raise small female children. I will get back to that in a moment....

Morally Condemned

... post-separation further, [Karla] continued to cohabit with [Lois] for reasons that she can address herself and no doubt to herself has addressed. She continued to engage in a relationship that society condemns and one that has been condemned through societies almost as long as man has been on this earth. She [Karla] is candid. I believe she is honest when she discusses her homosexual activities and her homosexual preferences.

[Frank], since he has been separated has also taken another mate, in actuality if not in legality. He has cohabited with Linda. And she candidly admits, as does [Frank], that she has shared his home and bed for the past several months.

One cannot help but wonder whatever happened to morality as it was taught in the religion of both of these people and in the Bible and the testament that you both appear to believe in. That aside, this isn't a lecture or an order about morality. This is a question of who should have custody of three small children.

Testimony and Tots

In her conversation with Doctor Rekers and in her testimony in this Court, [Karla] has indicated that she will terminate her relationship with [Lois] and she has stated her plan, if she obtains custody, to obtain a dwelling in the [downtown] area here in [Atlanta], to modify her working hours to maximize her time with her children. [Frank] has indicated his prospective future is to marry [Linda], to continue to have adequate shelter for the children and to proceed to raise the children in [Maine] or in that area with [Linda] being the surrogate mother.

There has been testimony on behalf of both parties that during the interim separation that the children albeit tiny have observed and know that [Linda] lives with daddy and have observed [Karla] and [Lois] in bed during visitation....

Bisexual Instability

This perhaps is one of the most difficult cases that can face a court. . . . It does no good to say [Karla] was wrong walking out because [Karla] had her reasons for [ending] a marriage that didn't work before she walked out. And it does no good to say [Frank] was put upon by having to care for these infants while [Karla] was doing her thing because the fact is the infants must go from today forward and be raised. . . . You award the children to the parent that you believe can do the best job from today forward in rearing the children.

Let's see what the evidence seems to indicate in that regard. Taking [Karla] first. . . . She has announced publicly her sexual preference. She has continued to maintain the lifestyle of that sexual preference at least until this hearing. She now indicates she will terminate it and change her residence in [Atlanta].

Now, let's suppose that happens and look at what the probabilities are of what the future holds for the three small children in [Karla's] custody. I have no doubt the children will be well cared for physically. I have no belief from the testimony that [Karla] is a promiscuous person or would live a heterosexual or homosexual existence that would be called loose in the vernacular street terms. There are those no doubt who will wonder how any homosexual existence could be anything but loose, but I think we are quibbling over terms.

If she [Karla] terminates her relationship with [Lois], this means a working mother will be raising three small children. Because she is an announced bisexual or homosexual it is unlikely that she will consummate a healthy future heterosexual marriage. I think then it is likely that one of three things will happen. Either she will continue her homosexual relationship with [Lois] or [Lois's] successor, should there be a successor, or she will remain alone and no doubt [be] quite bitter over her inability to obtain and to give the affection that her emotions say she should give and should have. This will mean her affection will have to be channeled entirely toward her children and there is some question in my mind whether that affection can be channeled without bitterness over circumstances also being communicated.

Further, let's assume, if we assume, that she takes a heterosexual partner who becomes her husband. Given the historical perspective of the failing two marriages, the homosexual release from the Air Force, and the homosexual affair from the perspective of [Lois] and [Karla], it would be curious if that arrangement could result in a substantial and stable male father figure coming into that home.

In addition, she will have to or would have to face the approbation

[sic] of the community directed against her as an individual because of her lifestyle, but more importantly directed against her children as her children in that lifestyle. [Karla's] desires are her business but as those desires affect the children those are the court's concern. How then and how would [Karla] cope with the social ostracism, the need to explain to the children at some time her own renouncing of the normal heterosexual role for children's parents, the probable two-person female role in the home? These are considerations that I see.

The Better of Two Evils?

[Frank] on the other hand would take a second wife. There's no evidence that that second marriage will be stable. . . .

I believe that [state] law indicates that between two equally fit parents the mother should have the preference and the custody of children in tender years. I have no difficulty with that in a normal case as an axiom of law. However, how is equally defined? In most simple terms, in which of the two homes will the children best thrive physically and emotionally until they are of age? Otherwise stated, which will provide them with the foundation of knowledge and values to best cope with their adulthood?

Based upon the testimony and appearance of counsel it is this Court's opinion that the best interest of the three minor children of [Frank] and [Karla] can be met by granting their permanent care, custody and control to their father, [Frank]. It is further this Court's opinion that in the event the future contracted marriage of the father in this case proves to be unstable, that either party may relitigate the issue of custody. It's the judgment of this Court that [Karla] pay the sum of twenty-five dollars per week per child as support to [Frank] to help to pay the care and cost of custody of the children. . . . And finally, this Court directs that the most liberal of visitation be taken between the parents to the end. That [Karla] has maximum contact with her children at any and all times and reasonable places. The Court is in recess.

What Is Sexual Abnormality?

Of all the forms of sexual abnormality, homosexuality attracts the most attention in current newspaper, radio, and television reports. This court case of Karla certainly received much local and national press coverage in 1979. As a result of unbalanced reporting, the public is perhaps confused about homosexuality.

Homosexual Rhetoric

So often, journalists have uncritically or deliberately adopted the terminology of the rhetoric of humanism.[2] As a result, homosexuality is not presented as an abnormality which inflicts suffering, loss of family fulfillment, and medical and moral consequences. The epidemic of venereal diseases among the homosexual population is not considered newsworthy to the authors of the humanistic rhetoric in our newspapers, radio, and televisions networks, even though the epidemic surpasses all other infectious diseases combined, and many new types of V.D. are presently untreatable.[3] Instead, we read and hear sympathetic reports of gay liberation rallies for "rights." Homosexuality is not presented as an unfortunate perversion, but as an alternate lifestyle. The promiscuous and perverted sexual behavior of these individuals in captivity is "objectively" reported by the media in terms of issues involving sexual freedom.

Captives to Confusion

What is the result of this media manipulation for the average person? The result is increased confusion. The problems of sexual confusion not only cause marital conflicts but also lead to a new generation of sexual captives among our youth. This captivity is actually a result of a false belief in determinism in human affairs. If a person believes that his sexual problem is predetermined, he feels trapped by it. If he feels trapped, he will not attempt to escape his condition. Because he gives up any hope for escape, he is a captive to his condition indeed. These captives then feel unjustly discriminated against because they believe that they have no more choice in the matter of their deviant sexual actions than the black man has a choice regarding his skin color. But this sexual captivity is really an illusion, because human free will and choice are realities, whether the person acknowledges it or not.

As the judge in Karla's case pointed out, the social consensus throughout the history of Western civilization has been that the heterosexual relations of a married couple are normal in the biological

2. See Michael Braun and George Alan Rekers, *The Christian in an Age of Sexual Eclipse* (Wheaton, IL: Tyndale, 1981), chapter 2, "The Rhetoric of Revolt: The Sexual Propaganda of Humanists."

3. According to numerous standard reports of the United States Center for Disease Control, Atlanta, Georgia.

sense, in the social sense, and in the moral sense. Any other sexual acts were recognized as abnormal sexuality. Therefore, a person's sexual relations with an animal are recognized as abnormal, and are called bestiality. Sexual relations with a dead body are recognized as abnormal, and are called necrophilia. An adult's sexual relations with a minor child are recognized as abnormal, and are called pedophilia. Sexual relations between two members of the same sex are recognized as abnormal, and are called homosexuality.

Similarly, sexual sadism is defined as "a sexual perversion in which sexual excitement and orgasm are dependent upon the infliction of pain and humiliation of others."[4] Masochism is defined as the "sexual perversion in which the individual derives sexual pleasure from the infliction of pain upon himself."[5] Fetishism is defined as "a pathological condition in which sexual impulses are habitually aroused and gratified by a nonsexual part of the body or a possession of the loved one."[6] Transvestism is the "strong desire to dress in the clothes customarily associated with the opposite sex" or the "sensation of sexual excitement when wearing clothes of the opposite sex."[7] Transsexualism is an abnormality in which a person identifies as a member of the opposite physical sex, as when an anatomically-normal male feels that he is a "woman trapped in a man's body."

Exhibitionism is defined as an abnormality in which the person exhibits his genitals in socially inappropriate places, for the purpose of his perverted gratification. Voyeurism is another sexual abnormality in which "sexual gratification [is] obtained from peeping, especially from watching people engage in sexual intercourse."[8]

Drawing the Line

In Western civilization, through the 1960s, the vast majority of the public recognized all these sexual conditions as abnormalities. The biological norm was recognized as the heterosexual relationship. The social norm was recognized as the married heterosexual relationship. And the moral norm was recognized as the loving, married

4. *Dictionary of Behavioral Science*, comp. and ed. Benjamin B. Wolman (New York: Van Nostrand Reinhold, 1973), p. 331.
   5. *Ibid.*, p. 228.
   6. *Ibid.*, p. 144.
   7. *Ibid.*, p. 391.
   8. *Ibid.*, p. 404.

heterosexual relationship. Any exceptions to these norms were recognized as perversions, sins, deviations, and abnormalities. In fact,
Webster's Dictionary defines "abnormal" as "deviating from the normal . . ."[9] and the *Dictionary of Behavioral Science* defines "abnormal"
as "diverging from the normal, not conforming with the general rule.
The term usually connotes pathology or deviation from what is considered psychologically adjustive."[10]

So the general public has understood conditions such as bestiality,
necrophilia, pedophilia, homosexuality, sexual sadism, masochism,
fetishism, transvestism, transsexualism, exhibitionism, and voyeurism to be abnormalities. These conditions are all clear deviations
from the norm of loving, married heterosexuality. In fact, heterosexual
promiscuity, marital infidelity, rape, and masturbation while looking
at pornography are other examples of sexual abnormality.

With a clear biological, social, or moral norm, it is a simple matter
for the logical mind to recognize sexual abnormality. Persons afflicted
with these abnormal sexual conditions have historically realized that
their sexual conduct is a deviation, a problem, a sinful yielding to
temptation, a conflict—that is, an abnormality. They have tended to
keep their sexual abnormality as secret as possible, or to reveal their
problem only to someone from whom they sought help—a spouse,
their clergyman, a physician, a psychologist, a marriage counselor,
a trusted friend, or God alone.

Morals and the Media Merchants

Since the advent of the rhetoric of sexual revolt in the 1960s and
1970s, many people are confused about what is and what is not an
abnormality. With the avalanche of press reports which use the terminology of the sexual "liberationists," the public is becoming confused about what is normal and abnormal. The popular press has
rapidly abandoned the terminology of normality—the words *fidelity*,
perversion, *deviation*, *pornography*, *permissiveness*, *promiscuity*,
adultery, *fornication*, and *pathology*. Instead, newspapers, radio
announcers, and television reporters have adopted the humanistic
vocabulary of manipulation and moral cover-up. We are bombarded

9. *Webster's New Collegiate Dictionary* (Springfield, MA: G. and C. Merriam, 1973), p. 3.
10. *Dictionary of Behavioral Science*, p. 2.

by the so-called objective reporting on homosexuality, which uses the terms *gay liberation*, *alternate lifestyle*, *sexual variation*, *affectional preferences*, *sexual freedom*, *sexist bias*, *gay minority rights*, and *homophobic bigotry*.

After more than a decade of this new humanistic propaganda from the media merchants, a growing segment of the public is confused about homosexuality. Now it is not unusual for a person to think, "Bestiality is abnormal, but I shouldn't speak of homosexuality as abnormal—it's just an alternative lifestyle." Others think, "We should have laws against pedophilia, but as long as the homosexual minds his own business, his life is none of my business." Still others think, "The very idea of necrophilia is sickening—it's clearly perverted. I used to feel that way about homosexuality, but now I've gotten over it."

Is "Consent" the Norm?

Now that homosexuals are attempting to gain respectability, what is the new norm for defining sexual normality and sexual abnormality? If loving, heterosexual marriage is not the norm, what is? If homosexuality can be acceptable, why aren't pedophilia, sexual sadism, or voyeurism considered normal? Where is the new dividing line? The humanistic rhetoric has merely changed feelings about homosexuality, but it has not given us a new logical norm against which we can judge what is normal and what is abnormal. Of course, that is the role of rhetoric—it cleverly changes feelings without being logical.

Homosexuality has been sold to the unwary public as a right between consenting adults. Karla and Lois were consenting adults in their homosexual indulgence. But was their consent enough? What about the consent of Frank, the legally married partner of Karla? He could have sued Lois for alienation of affection. What if Lois gave Karla one of the new untreatable types of V.D. which Karla could pass on to Frank? And what about the consent of the three little daughters? Did Karla really have the right to have sex with Lois?

Somehow, once homosexual acts are labeled as a right they are then perceived as something normal. But should society allow the life-threatening behavior of the sadist and masochist to continue, even if such behavior occurs between two consenting adults? Should it be a right for the sadist and masochist to enjoy their sexual exploits if society stops labeling their behavior "abnormal" or "perverted"? If the homosexual is granted this right, why not extend it to the sadist, masochist, necrophiliac, pedophiliac, fetishist, tranvestite, and exhibitionist? What is the new norm, if we abandon the historically-realized norm of loving, married heterosexuality?

The frightening thing about using this reductio ad absurdum logical argument against the defining of homosexuality as abnormal is this: The next calculated step of the sexual liberationists is exactly this—to force upon the public the idea that nothing is sexually abnormal! The gay liberationists have taken the deliberate ploy of pressing first for legislation to legalize the sexual behavior between two consenting *adults*. After they have succeeded in winning the emotional war of soothing the public's queasy feelings about homosexual activity among adults, the next planned step of the gay liberationists is to press for an elimination of laws of age discrimination (in the terminology of the rhetoric of revolt). This means that the gay activists are now beginning to press for the "rights of children" to engage in homosexual behavior with adults. This will be their battle to *legalize pedophilia*! Indeed, the very point of the humanistic rhetoric of sexual revolt is to discard any norm whatsoever. The humanistic press has already accommodated this movement by largely purging its vocabulary to eliminate words denoting norms, or normality.

In their crusade to eliminate the concept of sexual abnormality from the mind of the general public, the humanistic thinkers are waging a war for sexual liberation in the pages of magazines and newspapers and over the airways of television and radio. The *Humanist Manifesto* calls for the "right to divorce." We have witnessed their frontal assault upon the institution of marriage,[11] resulting in an escalating divorce rate. Their other major battlefield is in the area of homosexual behavior, which is just the prelude to their overall objective of removing the concept of sexual abnormality from the public consciousness. Once the concept of sexual abnormality has been erased from the public's mind and vocabulary, then "anything goes" in the humanistic utopia of amorality.

11. See Braun and Rekers, *The Christian in an Age of Sexual Eclipse*, chapter 6, "Marriage under Seige: Contemporary Challenges to a Faithful Marriage."

The Unisex Mentality Undermines
Family Life

Society can ill afford to have the attitudes of the likes of Karla become accepted by very many parents. Karla's blind, naïve, and destructive views on homosexuality can duplicate her own sexual problems in the lives of her children. Fortunately, the judge protected her three daughters from her. The girls are now living in a heterosexual family unit with their biological father. But even the mother's visits with her daughters on weekends can lead to sexual confusion for them if she trains them in the way she told me she would.

But Karla is an extreme case of a combination of ignorance about childhood sexual-identity development and personal rebellion against normal marital sexuality. She deliberately plans to deceive her children in the same way in which she is deceived. She is a captive to her own abnormality, and her blindness to her condition of moral depravity runs the risk of duplicating her own captivity in the lives of her daughters.

Most other parents do not plan to deliberately foul their children's potential for normal family fulfillment in marriage. Most parents realize the importance of normal heterosexual development, along with normal emotional adjustment, in their children.[12] Most parents want to know more about how they can eliminate possible homosexual temptations for their children. They want to know what is important to teach their child about sex. They want to provide a stable, loving, normal family life as a basis for their own child's normal sexual-identity development. They want their child to be sexually normal.

Fortunately the Karlas in this world are few. But the few of them are quite militant in their propaganda, even to the point of lobbying the professional groups whose members treat them.[13]

12. C. D. Broderick, "Normal Sociosexual Development," in *The Individual, Sex, and Society: A SIECUS Handbook for Teachers and Counselors*, ed. Carlfred B. Broderick and Jessie Bernard (Baltimore: Johns Hopkins, 1969), chapter 2. See also Leviticus 20:13; Romans 1:18 – 32; I Corinthians 6:9 – 11, 13b – 18; 7:10 – 11.

13. See Frank M. duMas, *Gay Is Not Good* (Nashville: Thomas Nelson, 1979), pp. 126 – 136 and 243 – 257, for a report and insightful critique of the way in which homosexual activists have manuevered politically within the American Psychiatric Association and American Psychological Association. See also George Alan Rekers, *Growing Up Straight: What Families Need to Know about Homosexuality* (Chicago: Moody, 1982), chapter 3.

Part *THREE*

Choices for Families

I was completely surprised when I looked up from the lectern. Streaming into the back of the large classroom, student demonstrators carried huge, hand-lettered signs that boldly proclaimed:

"Dr. Rekers' Research More Immoral Than the Vietnam War"

"Dr. Rekers Perpetuates Sex-role Stereotypes"

"Dr. Rekers Ignores Gay Children's Rights"

"Stop Dr. Rekers' UCLA Gender Project"

"Gay Children Are *Not* Mentally Ill"

Perhaps two dozen or more members of the gay student union on that large university campus had come to disrupt the workshop that I was invited to present for the continuing professional education of psychologists, family counselors, school guidance counselors, and teachers. The professional audience had paid a substantial registration fee to hear my all-day series of lectures and discussions on detecting and treating early signs of sexual-identity disorders in children. But the intruders chanted slogans and shouted insulting questions at me, making it impossible to proceed with my planned workshop.

A newspaper photographer wielded his flash camera around the room, catching various angles of the demonstration. (Later I learned that the reporters were from a well-known national newspaper for homosexuals. The demonstrators had brought the photographer with them.)

A number of the professionals in my audience attempted to reason with the demonstrators. "Can't you be quiet long enough to listen to what Dr. Rekers has to say? You haven't even given him a chance to present his case. We came here to hear him speak."

Another professional pleaded, "The university should be a place where academic freedom allows Dr. Rekers the opportunity to explain his research to us."

A demonstrator hotly replied, "Dr. Rekers' research should be stopped. He shouldn't be allowed to lecture here."

Finally, after patiently waiting a half-hour for the demonstrators to stop their interruption, another professional in the audience declared, "I paid a registration fee to hear Dr. Rekers lecture, and my ticket says that no one should be admitted to this university classroom without a paid ticket for admission. You students are stealing the class time I paid for. You are breaking the university regulations. I insist that you leave immediately."

An older professional proposed a compromise. "It's O.K. with me if the demonstrators stay in the room without a ticket so long as they stay quiet and let Dr. Rekers proceed with his lectures. Those of us who paid for our tickets should get first chance to ask Dr. Rekers questions, but if we have extra discussion time left over, I'd be interested in hearing Dr. Rekers answer some of the demonstrators' questions too."

At this point the demonstrators began arguing among themselves as to whether they should agree to the compromise. The professional audience debated the propriety of going along with any such compromise. I agreed to abide by the wishes of the paying audience. But the demonstrators quickly decided to reject the compromise offer and to continue their total disruption of my workshop.

In the ensuing turmoil, I quietly slipped out of the classroom through a side door and found a secretarial office, where I asked to use the phone to call the campus security office.

The security division responded by immediately dispatching a group of campus policemen in riot gear. They quickly restored order to the classroom by demanding that any individual without a ticket immediately leave the premises. They remained for a while to insure that my workshop session could get off to a proper start.

Some fifteen minutes or so after the campus police left the room, two of the former demonstrators slipped back into the room. One of the professionals demanded that they leave, but they promised to listen quietly. So the paying participants agreed to let the two stay.

By 4:00 P.M., I completed my workshop. Afterward the two students came up to me and expressed their appreciation for my talk and my treatment research program. One of them explained, "I doubt that our friends would have demonstrated against you if they had listened to you talk first." The other one said, "I wish my folks had taken me to see a doctor like you when I was young. It would have saved me a lot of suffering while I was growing up." He then talked to me for nearly an hour, explaining how he had grown up suffering the indignities of being called "sissy," "queer," and "fag" by other children, and how he wished he had a normal sexual identity.

I had been asked many questions that day by both the professionals and the homosexual activists. Some of the inquiries were genuine requests for information and others had been phrased by the activists in the most hostile sarcasm imaginable. To both types of questions, I attempted to provide calm and reasoned replies, in the hopes of dispelling misconceptions. The questions I faced that day included these:

What is a normal male identity for boys?

What is a normal female identity for girls?

What right do you have to influence children to be heterosexual instead of homosexual?

Aren't male and female roles outmoded for today's enlightened society?

Shouldn't boys and girls be reared equally and exactly the same?

In this section, one chapter is devoted to answers to questions about rearing boys to have a normal masculine identity. The other chapter answers questions for parents who need to know why and how to rear their daughters to have a normal feminine identity.

Each family today needs to make important choices between the unisex approach to rearing children and the normal approach of shaping male identities in boys and female identities in girls. These next two chapters offer practical advice for parents who choose to rear masculine boys and feminine girls.

6

Why Encourage Masculine Identity in Boys?

It was a rainy day, so Tommy, Mary, Billy, and Suzie were playing indoors. It was Suzie who suggested, "Let's play dress-up!"

The brothers and sisters scurried up to the attic where they pulled out the trunk of old clothes that they had permission to play with. This was a delightful set of make-believe costumes, including some of Dad's old suits, hats, pants, and shirts. Mom had stowed away a number of her dresses. There was the dress that she wore at her elementary-school graduation, as well as a few outfits she used to wear in high school.

Mary excitedly exclaimed, "Let me run downstairs and get my cosmetics set and my jewelry!"

For the rest of the dreary afternoon, the children dressed in various outfits and even put on a dramatic play, reminiscent of a soap opera.

In one of the skits, Tommy played the role of a pregnant woman. This was an especially hilarious drama in which Tommy stuffed pillows under a dress in order to look pregnant. He pretended that he went to a hospital, had a baby, and breast-fed the baby when bringing it home. A touch of realism was rendered when Mary carefully helped him put on lipstick, rouge, and eyeliner. Once Tommy had on the dress, these cosmetics, jewelry, and Mother's high-heeled shoes, he was the perfect picture of the little woman.

Mom and Dad were not quite sure what the plot was in the children's play-acting, but they smiled at one another as they overheard the hysterical giggling upstairs. Apparently the children were having a grand old time with the clothes. Dad commented to Mom,

95

"You know, those kids have a lot more fun with the old junk that we give them than they do with the expensive toys we buy them for Christmas."

This scene is probably repeated thousands of times in household upon household in American society. With slight variations, normal children, as they grow up, take on roles of "mommy" and "daddy" in their play. Sometimes boys will pretend that they are a girl or a woman. In the same way, girls will sometimes behave as boys, be "daddy" when playing house, or act like boys so often that they are referred to as tomboys.

When children explore male and female roles in this way, they are actually learning more about what it means to be a man or a woman. A boy who tries out the "mommy" role as well as the "daddy" role is learning the difference between the two. Trying out the opposite roles in a flexible way like this is part of the normal process of learning.

Sex-role Problems in Boys

There are rare instances, however, when a child's trying out of opposite sex roles becomes unusual. On the one hand, there are some boys who are so insistent on being supermasculine that they would always refuse to try out the role of "mommy" and even overdo a macho masculine role. These boys think that being masculine means that they must be violent and aggressive. They refuse to show any gentleness or sensitivity to other people. During the process of growing up, they somehow get a very distorted idea of what it means to be a male.

The opposite extreme is seen in boys who get carried away with the "mommy" role. These boys start rejecting their male role and might even insist, on occasion, that they are really girls! These boys overdo dressing in girls' clothes. They start telling their parents that they dislike boys' clothing. Some of them avoid boys' toys, and avoid playing with boys as well. At the same time, they begin to play more and more with girls only. It seems that they have developed an unhealthy fascination with wearing cosmetics, dresses, and women's wigs. They seem absolutely delighted if they can wear such items. Furthermore, they might adopt feminine-looking arm movements, body gestures, and mannerisms in their walk. In extreme cases they even say that they feel like a woman and that they want to grow up to bear children. Parents have reported problems like this in boys as young as three years old, while others report this kind of problem in children of all ages up to adolescence.

When boys persist in these kinds of feminine behaviors over a period of time (for six months to a year), they are likely to be referred to a child psychotherapist by their pediatrician, personnel at school, or their parents. An obvious question arises in the minds of adults around these children: Are these boys on the road to becoming a homosexual, a transvestite, or a transsexual?

Proper Masculinity or Phony Masculinity?

A lot of people are confused about what *is* proper masculinity. In the recent decade of women's liberation, stereotypes for both men and women have received close scrutiny. Now, more than ever before, we are aware of the unfair stereotypes that abound in our society. For example, it is unfair that men are not supposed to cry. It is an unfortunate, destructive, macho stereotype that insists that men should not show certain emotions in public. The saying, "Big boys don't cry," is not only an unnecessary limitation for boys but actually hampers their healthy personal development.

But just because there's a lot of phony masculinity perpetuated around us does not mean that there are no legitimate distinctions between men and women. Because a phony, macho masculinity has spread around does not mean that there is no such thing as a difference between a masculine role and a feminine role.

Let's think about this for a moment. Most little girls learn to copy a mothering role. This role includes pretending to deliver, breast-feed, and care for infants. Most little girls learn these mothering roles through the use of baby dolls. This is proper feminine role learning.

Sadly, some young boys may learn the wrong lesson from observing little girls taking care of baby dolls. Some little boys may begin to think that it is wrong for boys or men to take care of babies. This is not the lesson the boy should be learning, because fathers have an important role in cuddling and caring for babies too.

But what should the little boy learn about the masculine role that is different from the feminine role with regard to taking care of babies? The important lesson for the boy to learn is that he will not grow up with the biological possibility of having sex with a man to get pregnant, and therefore he will not be able to give birth to a child and breast-feed a baby. Those are the mother's roles. The little boy can pretend that he is "daddy" and he can pretend that he is loving his baby, changing his baby's diapers, feeding the baby, and playing with the baby.

In the same way, the little girls learn that there are biological reasons for the difference in the mother's role and the father's role. The little girls also learn that in our society they should wear modest clothing on their upper torsos. They learn that this is different from the clothing required to be worn by boys.

At the same time, a little boy learns that he would be ridiculed for wearing a dress regularly in public. The little boy learns that he can take his shirt off when he goes swimming, while girls in middle childhood are already required to wear tops while they go swimming in public.

These different assignments of male and female clothing do not violate human individuality. These different assignments of male and female clothing also do not impose an unfair restriction on children's development. They are realistic ways to help boys and girls to begin learning their unique sexual roles.

Male Identity

Most of all, it is important for parents to pay attention to a child's identity as a male or female. For example, many boys will put on an apron to help their mothers wash the dishes. In a sense, wearing an apron and washing dishes are considered somewhat feminine in our society. But it is not necessarily wrong for parents to encourage boys to be flexible enough to wear a kitchen apron while washing the dishes.

However, there are some boys, in rare cases, who should not be allowed to wear an apron to wash the dishes. These are boys who pretend regularly that they are really girls. When they put on an apron to wash the dishes, they may be pretending that they are really "mommy." If a parent suspects that this kind of thing is going on, the parent should be very careful to avoid such situations that might help the child practice the wrong sexual role. In such cases, the father should show the boy that he washes dishes, but that he washes dishes with the firm conviction that he is the "daddy" and *not* the "mommy." In this way, when both the mother and father share different household duties, they are teaching their children that a man can be secure as a man while he washes dishes and a woman can be secure as a woman while she washes the dishes.

We need to be flexible about these things, however. In some families, the boys grow up identifying with their fathers by never washing the dishes, just as their fathers never wash the dishes. There is nothing wrong for each family to work out their own role definitions as they go along in ways that are mutually satisfying. Some women do not want their husbands to "mess around" in *their* kitchens. And some husbands are content to mow the lawn and fix the car without having their wives intrude on those domains they protect. This is fine. Not everyone has to be the same. The important thing is that little boys need to be taught that being a boy is quite different from being a girl. And little girls need to learn that being a girl is quite different from being a boy. Every family has its own way of getting this across.

Is All Male Role-training Sexist?

There is a lot of talk these days about men's roles and women's roles. Some people insist that society is greatly changing its values regarding men's roles and women's roles. There is no solid scientific evidence that values of society have really changed all that much, except to eliminate some of the arbitrary limitations on women's entry into certain jobs.

We should not lose sight of the fact that little boys still need to be trained about what it is to be masculine. And little girls need to be trained about what it is to be feminine. Little children who have problems learning their proper sexual role are not likely to outgrow their confusion.[1] Instead, all studies of adults with serious sexual-

1. G. A. Rekers, "Atypical gender development and psychosocial adjustment," *Journal of Applied Behavior Analysis* 10 (1977): 559 – 571; G. A. Rekers et al., "Child gender disturbances: A clinical rationale for intervention," *Psychotherapy: Theory, Research, and Practice* 14 (1977): 2 – 11; G. A Rekers et al., "Sex-role stereotypy and professional intervention for childhood gender disturbances," *Professional Psychology* 9 (1978): 127 – 136; A. C. Rosen, G. A. Rekers, and P. M. Bentler, "Ethical issues in the treatment of children," *Journal of Social Issues* 34, no. 2 (1978): 122 – 136; G. A. Rekers and S. L. Mead, "Female sex-role deviance: Early identification and developmental intervention," *Journal of Clinical Child Psychology* 9, no. 3 (1980): 199 – 203.

identity problems show that the vast majority of them developed their sex-role problems while they were children.[2]

Even the so-called liberated parents who try not to teach their children about any differences between male and female roles will tell you that their own children remain quite traditional in their sex-role behavior. It appears that there still are very strong social pressures, from other children as well as from adults, which instill a traditional distinction between men's and women's roles. Children who fail to learn the differences in male and female role expectations suffer rejection from their group of little friends at school or in the neighborhood.

If a little boy takes on feminine attitudes, interests, and actions, other children will reject him. If his parents try to help him behave in a more masculine way (with or without psychological help), are they merely perpetuating a sexist attitude? If we advocate psychological treatment for the feminine boy, are we merely perpetuating male chauvinism?

It is true that boys outnumber girls with sexual-identity problems at a ratio of about 15 to 1.[3] Does this simply mean that society is unrealistically unflexible in its prescription of male roles for boys? Does this mean that professionals should spend all their time to alter society's intolerant expectations for boys, or is it the feminine boy who should be changed?

Who Am I?

Some boys may raise concern in their parents because they avoid normal playing with other boys their age and they spend most of their time alone or with girls only. Maybe they have never said that they prefer to be a girl but they just do not seem masculine.

There are other boys who prefer to play with girls but in addition have taken on certain compulsive patterns of wearing girls' attire and playing only with girls' toys. Maybe these boys have never called

2. Michael Braun and George Alan Rekers, *The Christian in an Age of Sexual Eclipse* (Wheaton, IL: Tyndale, 1981); Rekers et al., "Child gender disturbance."

3. G. A. Rekers, "Assessment and Treatment of Childhood Gender Problems," in *Advances in Clinical Child Psychology*, ed. Benjamin B. Lahey and Alan E. Kazdin (New York: Plenum, 1977), volume 1, chapter 7.

themselves a girl and maybe they have never said that they would prefer to grow up to be a mommy.

There are yet other boys who not only avoid masculine play and become obsessed with feminine play, but also persist in taking the role of "mommy" in games and state a desire to be a girl or a woman.

These may indeed be different degrees of the same problem. The problem may be a reluctance to take on a thoroughly masculine role. Some of these boys may be slow to take on a male role, without especially grasping on to a feminine role. Others may combine an avoidance of a boys' role with a strong adherence to a girlish role.

What becomes important, in any case, is for the parent to be alert to any sign that a boy might not be completely secure in his feeling of masculinity. Some boys are very convinced of their masculinity even though they do not like certain sports. That is all well and fine because not every boy has to be the same. Some boys are very secure in feeling masculine and in wanting to grow up to be a man, even though they do not fit the arbitrary stereotype of the all-American boy, which might imply some macho ways of behaving.

But sometimes it's difficult for a parent to really tell if the boy is happy and secure in his masculinity.

Underground Turmoil

It is a well-known fact that some boys with sexual-identity problems go "underground" with their problem as they approach later childhood and early adolescence. They become aware of the fact that their friends and family members would disapprove of obvious feminine actions. So they learn to behave in a superficially masculine way in public (suppressing their femininity) but underneath they feel a different way. Underground there is turmoil. Underneath they feel somewhat feminine.

Unfortunately, when a boy behaves one way but feels a different way, his personal adjustment is not what it should be. He cannot disclose his true self. This keeps him from becoming emotionally close to his friends. There is something to hide.

In fact, in secret, perhaps behind the locked bathroom door, the boy might use bathroom towels to put on his head and around his waist to pretend that he is really a woman. He observes his play-acted role in the mirror in the safe concealment behind a locked door. Mom and Dad may have no idea of his fantasy. This is especially true of boys eight years and older. Little boys, seven years and younger, are more likely to be detected as having such a problem because they are much more spontaneous in their actions.

Early Sexual Quandries

If a boy had qualms about his masculinity in late childhood, as he moves into adolescence his full sexuality becomes involved. Some boys may be inhibited in asking for a date. Their friends might call them "sissy," "queer," or "fag." And so the boy might feel very different inside. Children and teen-agers are perceptive and often observe sexual-identity confusion in a child much more readily than an adult might. In addition, some adult, practicing homosexuals have their eyes attuned to behavioral clues that indicate a boy is somewhat effeminate. For this reason, adult homosexuals may make sexual advances toward these somewhat effeminate boys.

With early homosexual experimentation, the boy may believe, "Well, I'm different anyway," and allow himself to experience homosexual arousal on repeated occasions.

Such a boy may translate his uncertain sexual identity into the quiet of a bedroom where he might compulsively masturbate, with feminine clothing as a stimulus. Or he might compulsively masturbate with a homosexual image in mind.

If a boy begins to develop a concept of himself as being at least partially female, this deviant sexual habit may grow and grow and grow and become a major focus and direction of his energies. He may feel different inside. He may feel that he cannot reveal this to his parents or close friends. But on his own, he pursues some feminine behaviors. Either he pursues feminine dressing in secret, or he pursues feminine sexual contacts, that is, contacts with males.

Some of these boys with an insecure sense of their own masculinity feel an emotional need to be closer to maleness. This becomes one of the reasons why sexual activity with another male is so attractive to them. They are using male sexual intimacy as a way to get close to a sense of maleness that they lack in their own identity.

Suffering by Girlish Boys

Some of the younger boys who have feminine features in their development run into trouble as they enter kindergarten. In many cases, when the boy first enters school, he is forced to interact with other boys and girls for the first time. For the first time he is behaving under the scrutiny of teachers, other parents, and the general community.

Other people might notice that these boys do not like to interact with other boys their age. In fact, they prefer to play quiet games with girls, and they often assume the female role in playing. Such boys are typically inept in sports. This means they have mastered very few athletic skills that would help them maintain a reasonable relationship with boys their age.

Some of these boys become fearful of going to school altogether because other children threaten them, reject them, withdraw from them, or take advantage of them. For these reasons, some effeminate boys prefer to play with children younger or smaller than themselves.

Even if we were not thinking, for the moment, about future problems such a boy may have, parents and psychologists (if necessary) should help such a boy to develop a normal play pattern and normal friendships with other boys and girls.

Emotional Emptiness

Boys who are not entirely comfortable with their masculinity suffer emotional problems. They are typically unhappy. Their near-obsession with feminine articles is very different from the kind of flexibility that other boys and girls display.[4] In fact, the evidence suggests that they are very similar to adults with sexual-identity problems who are severely depressed and who contemplate and try suicide.[5]

These boys are really confused about who they are. Their self-

4. G. A. Rekers, "Psychosexual and Gender Problems," in *Behavioral Assessment of Childhood Disorders*, ed. E. J. Mash and L. G. Terdal (New York: Guilford Press, 1981); G. A. Rekers, "Stimulus control over sex-typed play in cross-gender identified boys," *Journal of Experimental Child Psychology* 20 (1975): 136 – 148; G. A. Rekers and C. E. Yates, "Sex-typed play in feminoid boys versus normal girls and boys," *Journal of Abnormal Child Psychology* 4 (1976): 1 – 8; G. A. Rekers, H. Amaro-Plotkin, and B. P. Low, "Sex-typed mannerisms in normal boys and girls as a function of sex and age," *Child Development* 48 (1977): 275 – 278; A. C. Rosen, G. A. Rekers, and L. R. Friar, "Theoretical and diagnostic issues in childhood gender disturbances," *The Journal of Sex Research* 13, no. 2 (1977): 89 – 103; Rekers et al., "Sex-role stereotypy"; A. C. Rosen and G. A. Rekers, "Toward a taxonomic framework for variables of sex and gender," *Genetic Psychology Monographs* 102 (1980): 191 – 218.

5. See a review of the studies in Rekers et al., "Child gender disturbances"; Rekers, "Atypical gender development"; Rekers, "Psychosexual and Gender Problems," in *Behavioral Assessment of Childhood Disorders*.

concept is mixed up. They might rigidly hold to labeling themselves as different or as girls, in spite of reality, which demands that they be boys.

Playmate Problems

As a result, the boy faces the kind of rejection, ridicule, and isolation that is very unpleasant. These boys are frequently scapegoated by other children in very cruel ways. They must tolerate the indignity of insulting labels such as "sissy," "queer," or "fag." This makes their lives unhappy and uncomfortable. These labels also become self-fulfilling prophecies. As time goes on, if these boys are not helped, they become more and more isolated socially, they become more and more withdrawn, and they might even start acting in antisocial ways. These boys are often described as negativistic.[6] Some of the adjustment problems that are often associated with sexual-identity problems in boys are shyness, timidity, low self-esteem, feelings of rejection, detachment from other children, and inability to form close friendships with other children.

Why Help Is Needed

Obviously, much of the rejection and ridicule that these effeminate boys experience from other children stems from their feminine behavior. There's a vicious cycle—the child feels different and therefore acts differently; the playmates ridicule him; and the child feels all the more different, behaves all the more differently, and gets all the more ridicule.

These boys could get along better with other boys and girls if they could stop avoiding boyish play and if they could reduce the amount of their feminine play.

Although every boy should be free to develop his own pattern of interest, it is not adaptive for the boy to consistently avoid playing with cars and trucks and playing ball. Being inhibited like this makes the boy very inflexible. This means the boy is not especially able to perform the play activities that lead to happiness and social accep-

6. J. E. Bates et al., "Gender role abnormalities in boys: An analysis of clinical ratings," *Journal of Abnormal Child Psychology* 2 (1974): 1 – 16.

tance among other children. This is another reason why help is needed for the boy who is less than fully masculine.

Not all somewhat feminine boys will wear girls' clothing. But for those who do, this is a special problem that definitely requires psychological treatment. If the boy is uncertain in his masculinity, this may surface in a compulsion to wear the clothing of girls and women. This means that such a boy is risking a future temptation to become a tranvestite.

Adult male transvestites may have a certain acceptance of their physical sex as a male, but they develop a compulsive need to dress in women's clothing and to present themselves in a woman's role on occasion. Sometimes their cross-dressing becomes associated with sexual excitement.

Sad Consequences

There are serious disabling consequences that result from a compulsive wish to wear women's clothing. Adult men who have this habit find that it interferes with their normal heterosexual married life. On the one hand they may have a continuing sense of shame and a fear that their wives or children might find out about their cross-dressing. Or if their wives know about their cross-dressing, it can become a conflict in their married sex life. In addition, these men may threaten their social position by appearing in public in women's clothing. There are both legal and informal taboos against a man's wearing a woman's clothing in public places. This means that if this compulsion carries over into adulthood, it brings with it the possibility of social ostracism, personal and social isolation, and the threat of arrest, fines, or imprisonment for impersonating a woman.

Preventing Perversion

If a boy is developing a habit of wearing women's clothing, it is fully justified and, in fact, imperative that psychological help be offered to alter this disruptive behavior pattern. Adults find a cross-dressing compulsion to be at least awkward and often especially disruptive to their personal lives. This means that if we could eliminate this cross-dressing habit in children, we will be sparing them much misery in the future.

For this reason it is imperative for the mental-health profession to help youth with cross-dressing problems in order to prevent the kind of disturbing and disabling consequences that this problem presents in adulthood.

Boys who have problems adjusting to their male role are highly likely to grow up to be homosexuals, transsexuals, or transvestites. At the present time, there is no scientific way to predict which particular boy will be a homosexual as opposed to a transvestite or a transsexual. The best we can do is to predict that a boy who is uncomfortable in his masculinity is highly likely to be tempted by one of these sexual deviations in adulthood. Although we can predict a problem with a sexual deviation, we cannot predict exactly which deviation it will be.[7]

The available long-term studies indicate that boys with effeminate behavior turn out to be adult homosexuals at a high rate.[8] At the same time, in the studies of male adult homosexuals who have been asked about their childhoods, a common characteristic is effeminate behavior in the boyhood years.[9] The same is true of the studies of the childhoods of male transvestites[10] and male transsexuals.[11] The majority of adult male transsexuals and transvestites report that their

7. Rekers, "Atypical gender development."

8. H. Bakwin, "Deviant gender-role behavior in children: Relation to homosexuality," Pediatrics 41 (1968): 620 − 629; Richard Green, Sexual Identity Conflict in Children and Adults (New York: Penguin, 1975); P. S. Lebovitz, "Feminine behavior in boys: Aspects of its outcome," American Journal of Psychiatry 128 (1972): 1283 − 1289; B. Zuger, "Effeminate behavior in boys from early childhood: 1. The clinical syndrome and follow-up studies," Journal of Pediatrics 69 (1966): 1098 − 1107; B. Zuger, "Gender role determination: A critical review of the evidence from hermaphroditism," Psychosomatic Medicine 32 (1970a): 449 − 467; B. Zuger and P. Taylor, "Effeminate behavior present in boys from early childhood: II. Comparison with similar symptoms in non-effeminate boys," Pediatrics 44 (1969): 375 − 380.

9. Irving Bieber et al., Homosexuality: A Psychoanalytic Study (New York: Basic Books, 1962); R. B. Evans, "Childhood parental relationships of homosexual men," Journal of Consulting and Clinical Psychology 33 (1969): 129 − 135; E. R. Holemon and G. Winokur, "Effeminate homosexuality: A disease of childhood," American Journal of Orthopsychiatry 35 (1965): 48 − 56.

10. C. V. Prince and P. M. Bentler, "A survey of 504 cases of transvestism," Psychological Reports 31 (1972): 903 − 917.

11. Harry Benjamin, The Transsexual Phenomenon (New York: Warner Books, 1977); P. M. Bentler, "A typology of transsexualism: Gender identity theory and data," Archives of Sexual Behavior 5 (1976): 567 − 584; Richard Green and John Money, eds., Transsexualism and Sex Reassignment (Baltimore: Johns Hopkins, 1969).

effeminate behavior began in their earlier childhood years.[12]

We can reasonably conclude from the evidence, then, that difficulties in masculine identification in boys strongly predicts tendencies to homosexuality, transsexualism, or transvestism in adulthood.[13]

Reversing a Wrong Sexual Identity

I mentioned earlier that there are some boys who have trouble adjusting to their masculinity, although they do not actually say that they would rather be a girl than a boy. Then there are other children (for instance, Craig in chapter 2) who not only behave in a feminine way but also have a wrong sexual identity. These boys with a female identity need help, not only for all the reasons I have been discussing, but also for one more reason.

This final reason pertains to these boys' needs to have their wrong sexual identity corrected. The boys with a female identity are especially prone to be tempted toward homosexuality and transsexualism when they grow up.[14]

Dangers of Delaying

If parents and professionals delay in helping a boy with a feminine identity, they run the risk of letting the most extreme kind of sexual-identity problem develop—that is, the problem of transsexualism. A male transsexual is an adult who asks for surgery to change his body to that of a woman. One physician who has extensively studied transsexualism[15] has stated that there is virtually no treatment that might reverse such an identity problem for an adult. In fact, many professionals have given up the strategy of changing the person's attitude about his sexual identity and instead have tried to change

12. Green, *Sexual Identity Conflict*; J. Money and C. Primrose, "Sexual dimorphism and dissociation in the psychology of male transsexuals," *Journal of Nervous and Mental Disease* 147 (1968): 472 − 486; Prince and Bentler, "Survey of 504 cases of transvestism"; J. Walinder, *Transsexualism: A study of forty-three cases* (Copenhagen, Denmark, and Goteborg, Sweden: Scandinavian University Books, 1967); Zuger, "Effeminate behavior."

13. See reviews in Rekers et al., "Child gender disturbances"; G. A. Rekers and A. P. Jurich, "Development of Problems of Puberty and Sex Roles in Adolescents," in *Handbook of Clinical Child Psychology*, ed. C. E. Walker and M. C. Roberts (New York: Wiley, 1982).

14. See George Alan Rekers, *Growing Up Straight: What Families Need to Know about Homosexuality* (Chicago: Moody, 1982).

15. Benjamin, *The Transsexual Phenomenon*.

his body through surgery and hormones. For this reason there have been many unfortunate transsexuals who have had their male sex organs removed, even though there's no biological possibility for them to become reproductively a female.

Fortunately, there have been some recent cases of adult transsexuals who have been able to return to a normal sexual identity.[16] The most striking case was an example of a young man who was converted to the Christian faith and whose prayers resulted in a dramatic change to the normal sexual identity of a male. There have also been some other men who have received extensive behavior therapy and have been able to overcome their transsexualism.

Tragic Trouble

Unfortunately, transsexuals are deeply discontent and have severe conflicts. They usually have been able to attain only a minimum of educational success and are usually maladjusted in the work world.[17] They also have high rates of criminal and other antisocial behavior.[18]

In addition, two-thirds of these transsexuals have severe depression and 60 percent of them actually attempt suicide.[19] In desperation, many of them mutilate themselves by trying to cut off their male sex organs. The results of one study show that 18 percent of the transsexuals tried to cut off their penises and testicles and 9 percent actually accomplished this terrible thing.[20]

Overall, these men who have female identities are severely maladjusted emotionally, socially, and economically. They often face arrest, trial, and imprisonment for various criminal activities.

Because of these severe problems many physicians have gone along with the transsexuals' requests to be turned into women. They

16. D. H. Barlow, E. J. Reynolds, and W. S. Agras, "Gender identity change in a transsexual," *Archives of General Psychiatry* 28 (1973): 569 – 576; D. H. Barlow, G. G. Abel, and E. B. Blanchard, "Gender identity change in transsexuals: Follow-up and replications," *Archives of General Psychiatry* 36 (1979): 1001 – 1007; D. H. Barlow, G. G. Abel, and E. B. Blanchard, "Gender identity change in a transsexual: An exorcism," *Archives of Sexual Behavior* 6 (1977): 387 – 395.

17. J. Hoenig, J. Kenna, and A.Youd, "Social and economic aspects of transsexualism," *British Journal of Psychiatry* 117 (1970): 163 – 172.

18. *Ibid.*

19. I. Pauly, "Male psychosexual inversion: Transsexualism: A review of 100 cases," *Archives of General Psychiatry* 13 (1965): 172 – 181; Walinder, *Transsexualism.*

20. C. J. Dewhurst and R. R. Gordon, *The intersexual disorders* (London: Failli Tindall and Cassell, 1969); I. Pauly, "Adult manifestation of male transsexualism," in *Transsexualism and Sex Reassignment.*

give female sex hormones to these young men. These physicians also surgically remove the transsexuals' genitals and offer reconstructive cosmetic surgery to artificially develop a vagina and breasts.[21] This kind of medical treatment not only is highly experimental but also is subject to heavy criticism in the medical and nonmedical communities alike. There are major surgical, psychological, legal, and ethical problems posed by this kind of treatment.[22]

The cost of this kind of medical treatment can run into thousands and thousands of dollars. The transsexual young man is in a desperate position and can be easily exploited by medical professionals who charge high fees for such unusual sexual-reassignment therapy. Even after sex-reassignment surgery, many of these individuals never become normally adjusted. There are reported cases of some transsexuals who have changed their minds and want to go back to being males. Others become very promiscuous sexually in an attempt to validate their new sexual identity. Many of them become professional female prostitutes. In addition, a recent study found that in a large group of transsexuals, those who were given surgery were not found to be any better adjusted afterward than were those who were refused surgery.[23] For this reason, a major medical center hospital which performed many of these surgeries stopped performing that surgery because of the lack of evidence that it led to better-adjusted individuals.

An Absolute Necessity

Because of the extremely dire life circumstances of men with a female identity, and because their problems begin in childhood and adolescence, it is imperative to help these people while they are still youngsters. If parents and professionals can help a young boy or teen-ager to become comfortable with his male identity, they can help him avoid the pain, misery, and despair that he would face in adult life as a transsexual. It is much better to prevent transsexualism from occurring in adulthood than to allow it to develop unabated.

There is no way to sort the effeminate boys into categories so that we can predict which one will grow up to be a suffering transsexual or which one will become plagued by homosexuality or which one

21. Green and Money, *Transsexualism and Sex Reassignment.*
22. *Ibid.*
23. J. K. Meyer and D. J. Reter, "Sex reassignment: Follow-up," *Archives of General Psychiatry* 36 (1979): 1010 – 1015; "No surgery for transsexuals," *Time,* August 27, 1979, p. 73.

will be frustrated by transvestism. Instead, we need to help all young boys with masculine role problems in order to prevent their tragic fall into any one of these three lifetime patterns.

What Is Real Masculinity?

It is not necessary for all boys to be aggressive football players. It is not even desirable for all men to withhold natural expression of their emotions, even though this is a presumed male stereotype in North American and North European societies. Real masculinity involves a boy's or a man's full acceptance of his male physical sex status. It also involves reserving his sexuality for marriage with one woman (Matt. 15:19; I Cor. 6:9; 7:2). Real masculinity in a boy is not threatened when he might occasionally try on girls' clothing in a play situation.

For some boys, real masculinity involves their wholehearted participation in certain sports, but for other boys, masculinity is expressed in other kinds of interests.

In contrast, boys with problems in their sexual identity or with problems in taking on a masculine role are very rigid in their insistence on femininity. For example, adult male transsexuals have more rigid sex-role beliefs than do normal men and women.[24] Boys should not systematically avoid athletic games, even though these games may not be their favorite activity. They should be able to participate in the same games that other children participate in at their age. They need not be an expert. They need not be among the best players on a team. But they should be willing to participate if they are healthy enough to do so.

The Menacing Macho Myth

In our society, there is a macho myth that males should be socially insensitive and should inhibit public expressions of emotion. This is clearly a myth that inhibits full human development. It would not be right to teach boys to lose all their childhood tendencies for expressing feelings or for crying. It is not necessary to insist that

24. Thomas M. Kando, *Sex Change: The Achievement of Gender Identity by Feminized Transsexuals* (Springfield, IL: Charles C. Thomas, 1973).

your little boy behave like a stereotype of a macho character who systematically avoids any activity faintly reminiscent of a girl's activity.

But on the other hand, we must recognize that the homosexual, the transsexual, and the transvestite are socially handicapped people. It is for this reason that each of these types of adults has developed its own subculture. These sexually perverted individuals cannot totally blame society's macho myth for their need to meet together in their own groups and bars. There is such a thing as the macho myth but there is also such a thing as normal masculinity. And a normal male would not participate in the subcultures of the homosexual, transsexual, or transvestite.

True Masculinity

Even though there are some sex-role stereotypes that are quite arbitrary, there are, on the other hand, some standards for normal masculinity. There may be fewer rules for normal masculinity than there are rules for the macho myth. But nevertheless there is such a thing as an appropriate male role.

As a case in point, consider the physically normal young boy who has a desire to bear children and to breast-feed infants. This desire runs counter to normal masculinity. It is obviously impossible for the boy to fulfill these biological functions of motherhood. In such a case, the boy (not society) should change. We hear a lot of talk about how society needs to eliminate sex-role stereotypes. We hear the rhetoric about the unisex ideal. But the unisex mentality is a cruel farce, because there are some differences between the sexes. The word *unisex* actually implies that there is no difference between the sexes. Nonsense. Sex does make a difference.

Arbitrary Norms

It is true that there are some arbitrary male and female stereotypes in our culture. For example, in our society only women are allowed to wear skirts and dresses in everyday public life. Admittedly, this is an arbitrary distinction, in a way. But society does not need to change this distinction. This dress code does not hinder anyone's freedom to develop his potential. If a boy wants to wear dresses, it makes more sense for that boy to learn to adapt to his society rather than to insist that the society change its rule in this regard.

So there are some definitions of masculinity (for example, men do not wear dresses) that are arbitrary but benign.

The Real Difference

The radical feminist movement would have us believe that there are no legitimate distinctions between men and women, but a more realistic viewpoint is one where we recognize that there are some biological differences in men's and women's roles (see chapter 1). Motherhood has its distinctive feminine aspects, which are not arbitrarily assigned. But then again some of our dress codes (such as women, but not men, wearing dresses) are arbitrary but benign.

Finally, there is a third category that the legitimate women's movement has reminded us of—arbitrary and destructive sexual stereotypes. For example, the macho myth would have us believe that a doctor is a man and a nurse is a woman. But these are arbitrary classifications that *are* harmful. The stereotype of the male doctor and the female nurse should be eliminated in our society because it hinders the individual's freedom to develop.

Every boy should be trained in real and proper masculinity. This does not mean that the boy should be trained to live according to the menacing macho myth. However, just because there is a macho myth in our society does not mean that we should throw out all distinctions between men and women. The choice is not between unisex versus macho training for boys. Both of those extremes are equally wrong and equally destructive. We must achieve a balance between these two extremes. That balance is real masculinity, which should be affirmed in every young boy and every young man in order to prevent them from being strongly tempted by the sexual perversions of homosexuality, transsexualism, and transvestism.

7

Why Encourage Feminine Identity in Girls?

Remember Karla in chapter 4? She was the unwitting parent, the self-proclaimed bisexual, who went to court to argue for the custody of her three young daughters. When I interviewed her, she insisted that boys and girls should be reared the same way, with no distinction made between them. Karla was proclaiming the unisex propaganda. Actually, her attitude in this regard was potentially harmful for her children, particularly in the light of her unconcealed homosexual lifestyle. She was bent on teaching her daughters that there supposedly is no difference between being a female versus being a male. She was demonstrating this by her sexual relationships with other women. She was adopting a masculine sexual role herself by seeking sexual gratification from women rather than men. At the same time, she insisted that she would be teaching her children a unisex approach, which also denies the true essence of femininity and the true essence of masculinity.

When I wrote about Tommy, Mary, Billy, and Suzie early in the last chapter, I made the point that normal children will sometimes explore both male and female roles as part of their learning of those roles. It is also true that tomboyism in girls is more common in North American society than is effeminacy in boys. In fact, child-development studies suggest that 16 to 19 percent of all normal girls express a preference for masculine activities at some phase in their growing up.[1] For this reason, it is complicated for a parent to tell the differ-

1. D. G. Brown, "Sex-role preference in young children," *Psychological Monographs* 70, no. 14; whole, no. 421 (1956): 1 — 19; Marcel T. Saghir and Eli Robins, *Male and Female Homosexuality: A Comprehensive Investigation* (Baltimore: Williams and Wilkins, 1973).

ence between normal tomboyism and sexual-identity disturbances in girls.

Julie's Confusion

The reader will remember the case of Julie from chapter 1. Julie was a fourteen-year-old white girl from a rural background. Her mother had been divorced twice, and her family had made many moves during her childhood. Julie rarely had received any consistent affection from a father figure.

When Julie first appeared in my office, she was wearing a boy's shirt, a black leather jacket, blue jeans, and tennis shoes. She insisted that no one could force her to wear a dress.

Julie said that she felt like a boy and could remember wanting to be a boy for her whole life. She then asked if it was possible to transplant male sex organs onto her body.

Julie talked like a boy and had the gestures and mannerisms of a man. She also told me about her strong sexual interest in girls. She spent most of her time in a group of boys and included herself as "one of the boys" by referring to this group as "we." Whenever Julie talked about girls, it was in terms of romantic and sexual interest in them as girl friends.

At school, Julie flunked physical education again and again because she refused to participate on the girls' teams. She insisted on being on the boys' teams.

Julie also resented her physical change from a girl to a woman. She wore the black leather jacket tightly to hide her developing breasts. She always refused to wear a bra and she would never tell her mother when she needed feminine hygiene articles.

As a consequence of this rejection of her feminine role, Julie was rejected by most other teens her age and was accepted only by a group of socially misfit teen-agers. Julie was depressed most of the time and had thought about ways to commit suicide. She insisted that she felt that she'd rather be dead than remain a female.

Therapy Recommended

I recommended extensive individual psychotherapy and behavior therapy for Julie, using an approach that would attempt to alter her identity and sexual preferences to be in line with her physical status.

I recommended a videotape feedback and modeling approach to help her to become more flexible and appropriate in her gestures and mannerisms.

I further recommended that counseling also be directed toward the goal of showing Julie that the female role is not as limiting as she perceived it to be. I wanted her to understand that there are females who have achieved the kinds of things that she was interested in. For example, there are female recording artists with whom she could identify, instead of male recording artists.

Sex Education Needed

I found that Julie required extensive sex education and needed to learn about the impracticalities of sex-reassignment surgery. Julie had some unrealistic ideas about the possibility that male sex organs might be transplanted to her from some male who might prefer to be a woman instead of a man. The medical impossibility of this wish was pointed out to her.

Family Counseling Needed

In addition, Julie's mother needed counseling so she could better understand the seriousness of her daughter's adjustment problems and sexual-identity conflicts. The mother needed to learn that while Julie's early difficulties in adjusting to her female role may not have been obvious to adults in the past, the present evidence indicated that Julie's sexual-identity problems had been long-standing. Because Julie's sexual-identity problems had their roots in earlier childhood and because they had persisted for such a long time, her mother needed to learn the extent of Julie's problem. I informed the mother that Julie required immediate and extensive professional help.

I hoped, as well, that the mother would learn that it would be important to insure that her seven-year-old daughter received proper sex education to avoid some of the misunderstandings that Julie carried with her for many years and which contributed to her own sexual-identity problem.

An Unfortunate Dropout

I found a female psychotherapist for Julie, and Julie was very interested in meeting with her. But after Julie faced the fact that she could not be medically transformed into a man, she lost interest in coming to the clinic for visits. She decided that she did not want to change her sexual interests in other girls. If surgery to make her into a boy was not possible, then she angrily decided to "live with" being a "queer." She said, "I can't stand queers. It's just not normal. I can't stand the idea of a girl being a homosexual. And I'm mad that I'm a queer."

Julie had very intense feelings, and she continued to be so depressed that she was suicidal. Her psychotherapist tried to work with her at her own pace, but Julie dropped out of therapy. Many attempts were made to get Julie's mother to convince Julie to get the professional help she needed. But her mother was uninterested, and too busy developing a relationship with a new boyfriend. Julie continued to have extended phone conversations with her psychotherapist at some times of crisis, but decided not to come in for regular office visits.

Similarly, Julie was unmotivated to attempt to change her sexual interest in other girls, and she persisted in thinking that she could find happiness by pursuing her romantic interests in girls. Her captivity to homosexual and transsexual desires not only had yielded severe depression and suicidal urges, but also trapped her into thinking that her sexual proclivities could somehow yield future satisfaction.

Normal Tomboys versus Abnormal Tomboys

Julie's case points out the need for detecting her kind of problem at an earlier age, in order to prevent such a profound disturbance from developing. But will all tomboys find themselves in Julie's dilemma? No.

Then how can parents tell if a problem is brewing?

Julie is not a typical tomboy. A normal girl who is known as a tomboy for a certain phase in her life is not so rigid, excessive, and compulsive in performing masculine roles. A normal tomboy does not take on such a comprehensive male identity.

Tomboyism can often be a normal phase of feminine development. But a small percentage of tomboys are genuinely unhappy about being girls.[2] For this minority, the masculine behavior is linked to sexual-identity confusion. It is often difficult for a parent to know if his or her daughter is an example of normal or abnormal tomboyism. The reason is that normal and abnormal tomboys often behave the same way. The only difference is that the abnormal tomboy would truly rather be a boy than a girl.

What are some of the differences between normal tomboys and abnormal tomboys? Normal tomboys may prefer masculine activities as a child but they accept their basic female identity. Normal tomboys usually pass through this stage and become more feminine in their interests as adolescence begins.

In contrast, abnormal tomboys persist in their masculine roles as they enter adolescence. They do not pass out of the phase. Instead, they are on the road to becoming an adult homosexual or transsexual.[3] Abnormal tomboys might also ask to be called by a boy's name and imply that they are male instead of female.

Most normal tomboys are girls who are feminine in their earlier childhood and pass into a masculine role phase in later childhood, only to pass back to a feminine role as they become teen-agers. In contrast, adult female transsexuals report that their masculine interests began at a very early age, perhaps at three or four years old. So the normal tomboy is more likely to be feminine in her role at ages three, four, five, and six, and may pass into a tomboy phase after that. But the abnormal tomboys started out behaving in a masculine role at their youngest childhood ages.

Preventing Female Perversion

Psychologists and psychiatrists have found it very difficult to treat women with severe sexual-identity problems. Only in one instance has an adult female transsexual been successfully treated to accept a female role.[4] As a consequence, it is important to detect the differ-

2. R. Green, "Intervention and prevention: The child with cross-sex identity," in *The Prevention of Sexual Disorders: Issues and Approaches* ed. C. B. Qualls, J. P. Wincze, and D. H. Barlow (New York: Plenum, 1978).

3. R. Green, "Sexual identity: Research strategies," *Archives of Sexual Behavior* 4 (1975): 337 – 352; Saghir and Robins, *Male and Female Homosexuality.*

4. C. W. Davenport and S. I. Harrison, "Gender identity change in a female adolescent transsexual," *Archives of Sexual Behavior* 6 (1977): 327 – 340.

ence between normal and abnormal tomboyism in young girls in order to prevent the strong temptations toward homosexuality and transsexualism in adulthood.[5] It is important to avoid having girls grow up with the desire to be surgically transformed into a male, because many physicians would go along with that abnormal request.

A much better strategy is to find girls with sexual-identity problems and offer them help before they are tempted toward homosexuality or transsexualism in adulthood. I recently published an article about the first case of an abnormal tomboy who was treated to adapt to a normal female role.[6] This is a much preferred strategy than to wait and allow sexual-identity problems to persist into adulthood.

Abnormal Tomboys Grow Up

The overwhelming majority of female transsexuals report that they wanted to be a male ever since they were very young children.[7] For example, in one series of cases, 100 percent of these adult women transsexuals felt as though they belonged to the opposite sex before they were teen-agers, and 92 percent of them were tomboys as girls.[8]

Female transsexuals show evidence of abnormal tomboyism usually by the age of three or four and most certainly by age seven or so.[9] Most of the parents of female transsexuals have reported that they became aware that something was wrong with their girls in early childhood.[10]

What were these abnormal tomboys like? They were very active,

5. L. E. Newman, "Transsexualism in adolescence: Problems in evaluation and treatment," *Archives of General Psychiatry* 23 (1970): 112 – 121; I. Pauly, "Female transsexualism: Part II," *Archives of Sexual Behavior* 3 (1974): 509 – 526; C. B. Qualls, "The Prevention of Sexual Disorders: An Overview," in *The Prevention of Sexual Disorders: Issues and Approaches* chapter 1; G. A. Rekers et al., "Sex-role stereotypy and professional intervention for childhood gender disturbances," *Professional Psychology* 9 (1978): 127 – 136; G. A. Rekers and S. L. Mead, "Female sex-role deviance: Early identification and developmental intervention," *Journal of Clinical Child Psychology* 9 (1980): 199 – 203.

6. G. A. Rekers and S. L. Mead, "Early intervention for female sexual identity disturbance: Self-monitoring of play behavior," *Journal of Abnormal Child Psychology* 8 (1979): 405 – 423.

7. H. Benjamin, "Clinical aspects of transsexualism in male and female," *American Journal of Psychotherapy* 18 (1964): 458 – 469; Richard Green, *Sexual Identity Conflict in Children and Adults* (New York: Basic Books, 1974); I. Pauly, "Female transsexualism: Part I," *Archives of Sexual Behavior* 3 (1974): 487 – 507.

8. J. Walinder, *Transsexualism: A study of forty-three cases* (Copenhagen, Denmark, and Goteborg, Sweden: Scandinavian University Books, 1967).

9. Pauly, "Female transsexualism."

10. Benjamin, "Clinical aspects of transsexualism."

and often displayed physical aggression, particularly against boys.[11] Almost all of them were called a tomboy.[12] They preferred playing with boys[13] and they preferred wearing boys' clothing.[14] Most of them avoided playing with dolls[15] and all of them preferred playing with boys' toys rather than girls' toys.[16] The majority of them identified with their fathers rather than with their mothers.[17]

These abnormal tomboys found that the onset of puberty was very traumatic for them. Almost all of them were repulsed by the development of their breasts[18] and they often reacted to this development by binding their breasts.[19] In the same way, these abnormal tomboys were repulsed by menstruation,[20] they despised their own sexual organs[21] and many of them requested medical procedures to transform them into a boy.[22] Most of these abnormal tomboys reported that they became sexually attracted to very feminine girls when they were in their early teens.[23]

What Happens When Abnormal Tomboys Grow Up?

Some of these abnormal tomboys became transsexuals when they grew up. But others grew up to be homosexuals or transvestites. A few grow up to be heterosexuals, but they are in the minority. Research has found that the majority of female adult homosexuals report that

11. J. Money and J. G. Brennan, "Sexual Dimorphism in the Psychology of Female Transsexuals," in *Transsexualism and Sex Reassignment*, ed. Richard Green and John Money (Baltimore: Johns Hopkins, 1969).

12. Money and Brennan, "Sexual Dimorphism"; J. H. Vogt, "Five cases of transsexualism in females," *Acta Psychiatria Scandinavia* 44 (1968): 62 – 88; Walinder, *Transsexualism*.

13. Money and Brennan, "Sexual Dimorphism"; Pauly, "Female transsexualism."

14. Green, *Sexual Identity Conflict*; Money and Brennan, "Sexual Dimorphism"; Vogt, "Five cases of transsexualism."

15. Money and Brennan, "Sexual Dimorphism."

16. Green, *Sexual Identity Conflict*; Pauly, "Female transsexualism"; Vogt, "Five cases of transsexualism."

17. Pauly, "Female transsexualism."

18. Benjamin, "Clinical aspects of transsexualism"; Money and Brennan, "Sexual Dimorphism"; Pauly, "Female transsexualism"; Walinder, *Transsexualism*.

19. Money and Brennan, "Sexual Dimorphism"; Pauly, "Female transsexualism."

20. Benjamin, "Clinical aspects of transsexualism"; Money and Brennan, "Sexual Dimorphism."

21. Pauly, "Female transsexualism"; Walinder, *Transsexualism*.

22. Walinder, *Transsexualism*.

23. Pauly, "Female transsexualism."

they wished that they were a boy when they were young, and preferred playing with boys and with boys' toys rather than with girls and girls' toys.[24] Adult lesbians are more likely to have identified with their fathers rather than their mothers, and a majority of them became aware of homosexual temptations before the age of fourteen. The only major difference between the abnormal tomboys who grew up to be homosexuals rather than transsexuals is that as a child the girls who grew up to be lesbians rarely had a desire for a surgical sex change.

More than two-thirds of adult female homosexuals have reported that they were tomboys as children. This is in comparison with 16 percent of normal heterosexual women who were used as a control group. Nearly all adult female transsexuals recalled being tomboys in their youth. So this is a big difference. Sixteen percent of heterosexuals, 67 percent of female homosexuals, and nearly 100 percent of female transsexuals were tomboys when they grew up.

The tomboy stage persisted from childhood into the teen-age years or into adulthood for approximately one-half of all the homosexual women, but for none of the heterosexual women.[25] Another interesting comparison is that female adult homosexuals who were tomboys reported that when they were little girls they disliked playing with dolls and avoided it as much as possible, while female heterosexual women who were tomboys did not avoid playing with dolls.[26] This means that parents of tomboy daughters should look for this distinction. Did your girl avoid playing with dolls, along with being a tomboy for a long period of her childhood?

Because tomboyism persists into adolescence and adulthood[27] in cases of female transsexualism and female homosexuality, the length of the tomboy phase is very important to consider as well.

Which Perversion Results

Although it would be convenient to know whether a particular tomboy will become a homosexual or a transsexual, there's no sci-

---

24. Saghir and Robins, *Male and Female Homosexuality.*
25. *Ibid.*
26. *Ibid.*
27. Green, "Sexual identity: Research strategies."

entific evidence at the present time to make this differentiation,[28] and such a study might be unethical to conduct anyway. However, there are some researchers who are trying to collect this kind of longitudinal information on tomboys.[29]

But as is true with boys, it is not possible to tell whether a particular abnormal tomboy will become a transsexual or a homosexual. Adult homosexual and transsexual females report very similar childhood patterns of abnormal tomboyism. All we can predict is that a girl who is an abnormal tomboy will be highly likely to suffer the temptations of either homosexuality or transsexualism in adulthood (in the same way that we can make only this general prediction for boys).[30] Not every girl with a history of abnormal tomboyism will invariably succumb to homosexual or transsexual temptation in adulthood, but we can conclude that there's an exceptionally high probability that she will be tempted by these sexual deviations.

So abnormal tomboys should be helped by parents, cooperating with psychologists and psychiatrists, in order to prevent a strong temptation toward homosexuality or transsexualism when these girls grow up into the teen-age and adult years. But there are even more reasons why such a girl should be treated.

Preventing Emotional Problems

Not only do abnormal tomboys grow up to have pronounced temptations toward homosexual behavior or transsexualism, but they also are very likely to experience other severe adjustment problems. Sixty-nine percent of female transsexuals suffer severe depression.[31] In many cases, their depression is accompanied by thoughts of suicide

28. R. C. Kolodny, "Ethical Issues in the Prevention of Sexual Problems," in *The Prevention of Sexual Disorders: Issues and Approaches*.

29. S. J. Bradley et al., "Gender identity problems of children and adolescents," *Canadian Psychiatric Association Journal* 23 (1978): 175 – 183; Green, *Sexual Identity Conflict*.

30. H. Bakwin, "Deviant gender-role behavior in children: Relation to homosexuality," *Pediatrics* 41 (1968): 620 – 629; P. S. Lebovitz, "Feminine behavior in boys: Aspects of its outcome," *American Journal of Psychiatry* 128 (1972): 1283 – 1289; B. Zuger, "Effeminate behavior present in boys from early childhood: I. The clinical syndrome and follow-up studies," *Journal of Pediatrics* 69 (1966): 1098 – 1107; B. Zuger, "Effeminate behavior present in boys from childhood: Ten additional years of follow-up," *Comprehensive Psychiatry* 19 (1978): 363 – 369.

31. Pauly, "Female transsexualism"; Walinder, *Transsexualism*.

and suicide attempts as well as by psychiatric hospitalization.[32] The majority of female transsexuals have serious personality disorders, often psychopathic personalities.[33] Forty-four percent of transsexual women are involved in antisocial behaviors such as thievery, armed robbery, and alcoholism. It is very common for these women to score on psychological tests as psychopathic deviants.[34] This is an interesting finding, in the light that abnormal tomboys are also very aggressive.[35]

Emotional Disturbance of Female Homosexuals

Studies of adult lesbians who are under psychiatric care consistently report a high incidence of psychiatric disorders ranging from neuroticism and personality disorders[36] to schizophrenia.[37] When equated with heterosexual women for psychiatric diagnosis, lesbian women have a much higher incidence of alcohol and drug abuse.[38] Not only that, but homosexual women are also more likely to have a more unstable work record when they are compared with heterosexual control groups.[39]

Although the incidence of psychiatric disorders is lower in lesbians who are recruited to be research subjects from gay liberation organizations, it should be pointed out that these studies are biased in that the subjects are probably more vocal, better educated, and less socially isolated than homosexuals in general.

32. Pauly, "Female transsexualism"; Walinder, *Transsexualism*.

33. Pauly, "Female transsexualism."

34. H. B. Roback et al., "Psychopathology in female sex-change applicants and two help-seeking controls," *Journal of Abnormal Psychology* 85 (1976): 430 – 432; A. C. Rosen, "Brief report of MMPI characteristics of sexual deviation," *Psychological Reports* 35 (1974): 73 – 74.

35. M. W. Kremer and A. H. Rifkin, "The early development of homosexuality: A study of adolescent lesbians," *American Journal of Psychiatry* 126 (1969): 91 – 96; Money and Brennan, "Sexual Dimorphism."

36. L. K. Gluckman, "Lesbianism: A clinical approach," *New Zealand Medical Journal* 65 (1966): 443 – 449.

37. H. E. Kaye et al., "Homosexuality in women," *Archives of General Psychiatry* 17 (1967): 626 – 634.

38. D. W. Swanson et al., "Clinical features of the female homosexual patient," *Journal of Nervous and Mental Disease* 155 (1972): 119 – 124.

39. F. E. Kenyon, "Studies in female homosexuality: IV. Social and psychiatric aspects," *British Journal of Psychiatry* 114 (1968): 1337 – 1350.

Disturbance in Nonpatient Homosexuals

Although some studies have not found the difference,[40] other studies have found that nonpatient lesbians are more susceptible than heterosexuals to dropping out of college, to depression, to suicide attempts, and to alcohol and drug abuse.[41] They're much more likely to report a previous nervous breakdown, often related to depression,[42] than are the members of a control group. The most common forms of psychopathology in nonpatient homosexuals are depression and anxiety.[43] In a study of professionally-employed homosexual women who were neither members of a gay liberation group nor psychiatric patients, the lesbian women were more likely to score higher on the schizophrenia scales of a personality test than were the heterosexuals in the control group.

Although there is a range of psychological adjustment found in lesbians, psychopathology is often found in conjunction with their homosexuality. At the present time, it is not possible to predict which abnormal tomboys will eventually grow up to be sexually deviant with additional psychopathology, as opposed to being just sexually deviant.

Therefore, parents should seek professional help for their abnormal tomboys, not only to prevent the possibility that they may become homosexual or transsexual, but also to prevent these other severe forms of psychological disorder which typically accompany sexual deviation in females. But there is even one more reason to help abnormal tomboy girls.

Help for Current Conflicts

Abnormal tomboys simply are not as flexible as normal girls in their play.[44] They need to learn to increase the range of their behav-

40. For example, N. L. Thompson, B. R. McCandless, and B. R. Strickland, "Personal adjustment of male and female homosexuals and heterosexuals," *Journal of Abnormal Psychology* 78 (1971): 237 – 240.

41. Saghir and Robins, *Male and Female Homosexuality.*

42. Kenyon, "Studies in female homosexuality."

43. *Ibid.*

44. G. A. Rekers and C. E. Yates, "Sex-typed play in feminoid boys versus normal boys and girls," *Journal of Abnormal Child Psychology* 4 (1976): 1 – 8.

iors to include feminine activities.[45] Because of their rigid tomboy behavior, they sometimes experience peer ridicule and rejection.[46] The effects of this social alienation can be psychologically harmful. The physical aggressiveness of abnormal tomboys also results in some of their social maladjustment. Aggression is less likely to be tolerated in girls than in boys.[47] It is true that excessive physical aggression is maladaptive in boys, but it is equally or more maladaptive in girls.

In a study of twenty-five teen-age girls involved in homosexuality, it was found that all of them had significant psychological disorders and twelve of them were diagnosed as aggressive personalities.[48] One-third of these girls had threatened or attempted suicide, revealing their serious personal maladjustment.

Similarly, when adult female homosexuals are compared with adult heterosexuals in control groups, it is found that the lesbian women are more likely to report having had an unhappy childhood.[49]

These abnormal tomboys experienced a lot of conflict about their self-concept. They are torn between their desire to be a boy and the social demands of their daily life that require feminine roles.[50] It is generally concluded that abnormal tomboys need psychological help because of the psychological conflicts they experience as a result of their desire to be a member of the opposite sex.

Helping Parents of Abnormal Tomboys

Professionals have an ethical responsibility to help the parents with abnormal tomboys. Sometimes families need help in adjusting the family factors that contribute to abnormal tomboyism.

Much research remains to be done to address the question of what family factors encourage abnormal tomboyism. However, the adulthood reports of female transsexuals and homosexuals suggest that the parents have an important role for the individuals. In chapter 3, we saw that the father is the parent who is more actively

45. Rekers and Mead, "Early intervention."
46. Saghir and Robins, *Male and Female Homosexuality.*
47. Money and Brennan, "Sexual Dimorphism."
48. Kremer and Rifkin, "Early development of homosexuality."
49. Kenyon, "Studies in female homosexuality."
50. Pauly, "Female transsexualism."

involved in the sex-typing of his children.[51] The father appears to be closely related to the development of abnormal tomboyism. Some female transsexuals, as children, viewed their mothers as having low status and consequently took on a masculine, protective role toward their mothers. In other words, if a girl's mother is not properly protected by a father or father figure, a young daughter may abnormally take on a masculine, protective role toward the mother. In some cases the father might even encourage his daughter's adoption of this fatherly role towards the mother. And in some cases the father approves his daughter's tomboyism.[52]

Other studies have found that female transsexuals grew up viewing their mothers as being emotionally disturbed and needing protection from their fathers.[53] The fathers of female transsexuals were much more physically abusive, overly masculine, alcoholic, or otherwise emotionally disturbed than is usual. It has been found that female transsexuals suffered from higher degrees of father absence and father alcoholism than did other women.[54]

It is a sad fact, then, that the fathers of female transsexuals often encourage masculinity in their daughters. These fathers are often distant from their daughters, either physically or psychologically. Or these fathers may be openly rejecting and abusive toward their daughters and wives, providing a motivation for the daughter to take a masculine role toward the mother.

Studies of adult lesbians have also found disordered family relationships. Parents of female homosexuals are reported to be often involved in marital conflict[55] and are more likely than most parents to obtain a divorce before their daughters reach the age of ten years.[56] The fathers of lesbians are usually reported as being hostile or

51. B. I. Fagot, "Sex differences in toddler's behavior and parental reaction," *Developmental Psychology* 10 (1974): 554 − 558; J. Z. Rubin, F. J. Provenzano, and Z. Luria, "The eye of the beholder: Parents' views on sex of newborns," *American Journal of Orthopsychiatry* 44 (1974): 512 − 519.

52. Walinder, *Transsexualism.*

53. Pauly, "Female transsexualism," parts 1 and 2.

54. Walinder, *Transsexualism.*

55. Kenyon, "Studies in female homosexuality"; J. Loney, "Family dynamics in homosexual women," *Archives of Sexual Behavior* 2 (1973): 343 − 350; M. Siegelman, "Parental background of homosexual and heterosexual women," *British Journal of Psychiatry* 124 (1974): 14 − 21.

56. Saghir and Robins, *Male and Female Homosexuality.*

detached[57] and the father-daughter relations are usually distant and lacking in affection.[58] When fathers of homosexual women are compared with fathers of heterosexual women, it is found that the fathers of the lesbians are more likely to be alcoholic and physically abusive[59] and their daughters often fear them. These fathers tend to be overly possessive and inhibit their daughters' development as women.[60]

57. Kremer and Rifkin, "Early development of homosexuality"; E. Bene, "On the genesis of female homosexuality," *British Journal of Psychiatry* 111 (1965): 815—821.

58. R. H. Gundlach and B. F. Riess, "Self- and Sexual Identity in the Female: A Study of Female Homosexuals," in *New Directions in Mental Health*, ed. Bernard F. Riess, 2 vols. (New York: Grune and Stratton, 1968); K. Poole, "The etiology of gender identity and the lesbian," *The Journal of Social Psychology* 87 (1972): 51—57; Siegelman, "Parental background."

59. Swanson et al., "Clinical features of the female homosexual."

60. Kaye et al., "Homosexuality in women."

Part FOUR

Challenges Facing Families

My two areas of professional specialization within psychology are clinical child psychology and marriage counseling. As you might well imagine, the two go very well hand-in-hand. In fact, putting the two specializations together in a single title would yield the term *family psychologist* or *family therapist*. Many physicians specialize in a branch of medicine recently designated as "family practice," and it would make similar sense for me to describe my clinical work in psychology as family practice.

Of course, my work in family counseling goes beyond the initial step of identifying family problems, because I am most interested in helping families solve their problems and face their growing challenges in this complex world. Two kinds of distinct challenges face families when it comes to the task of shaping children's sexual identities. These two challenges can be represented by these questions:

What can I do to correct a sexual-identity problem that has developed in my child?

What can I do as a parent to prevent a sexual-identity problem from developing in my child?

In psychology, we refer to the first challenge by the term *treatment*, and we call the second challenge *prevention*.

The question about treatment requires a separate chapter for boys and another for girls. Even parents interested only in the challenge of prevention can learn some pointers in these two chapters about correcting sexual-identity problems in children. Then I will conclude this book with a summary chapter about prevention of sexual-identity problems by considering what is involved for parents who want to shape masculine identities in boys and feminine identities in girls.

8

Correcting Sexual-identity Problems in Boys

Where do sexual-identity problems begin? That question was the subject of chapter 2, where I directed attention to the importance of the family backgrounds of children troubled by sex-role deviations. I introduced my discussion of the importance of the child's families by describing two children in that chapter. But I stopped short of telling their whole stories. Now I'll return to the cases of Craig and Becky to describe how I helped them and their families.

What Ever Happened with Craig?

Do you remember Craig? He was the four-year, eleven-month-old boy referred to me ten years ago for his severe sexual-identity problem. His early childhood development pattern was the same as that reported by a large number of adult male homosexuals, transvestites, and transsexuals.

For more than a year, Craig had been telling everyone around him that he wanted to be a girl, that he wanted to grow up to be a "mommy," to deliver babies, and to breast-feed them. He compulsively put on girls' dresses, lipstick, and other cosmetics, in order to make himself look like a female. If he could not find a dress to wear, he would frequently use his creativity to improvise and pretend that he was wearing a dress. For example, he would get one of his father's T-shirts and pretend that it was a dress, and he would put a mop or towel over his head to pretend that he had long hair.

A Feminine Boy

Craig behaved in a way that was a caricature of femininity. He frequently displayed a weak, limp wrist and he swayed his hips when he walked. The ways in which he held his arms and the delicate ways he carefully folded his legs were all an imitation of a hyperfeminine role. It was remarkable how he could mimic all these subtle feminine behaviors as though he were a woman.

Not only did Craig avoid the rough-and-tumble games of other boys his age, but he also preferred to play only with girls. His favorite game was to play house. He would take the role of "mother" and insist that one of the girls play the part of "father."

The physician who had referred Craig to me for psychological treatment had indicated that Craig was physically normal in terms of currently available methods of biomedical testing.[1] I had Craig evaluated by a specialist in pediatric endocrinology and genetics who found that Craig was a normal male genetically and physically, with the exception of one undescended testicle. However, this is not a physical condition that would automatically cause a female sexual identity.[2]

The Parents' Moral Concerns

Craig had Christian parents who were concerned that their boy might become a homosexual or a transsexual if they did not obtain help for his sexual-identity problem.[3] Craig's mother told me that she had been praying for some time for a solution to her son's problem. She learned about my new program on childhood gender problems from a local television talk show and she told me that she immediately felt that this was a direct answer to her prayer. When she brought the family in for the initial consultation, she expressed hope that I could help Craig be satisfied and comfortable about being a boy. She and her husband wanted Craig to grow up with the potential of having a normal heterosexual marriage, and the family fulfillment that comes with normal married life.

1. G. A. Rekers et al., "Genetic and physical studies of male children with psychological gender disturbance," *Psychological Medicine* 9 (1979): 373 – 375.

2. G. A. Rekers, "Psychosexual and Gender Problems," in *Behavioral Assessment of Childhood Disorders*, ed. E. J. Mash and L. G. Terdal (New York: Guilford Press, 1981).

3. G. A. Rekers, "Atypical gender development and psychosocial adjustment," *Journal of Applied Behavior Analysis* 10 (1977): 559 – 571.

At the time that Craig was brought to me for treatment at the UCLA Psychology Department, I knew that no psychologist or psychiatrist had ever scientifically demonstrated effective treatment for reversing such a pronounced cross-sexual identity in a child of any age. I also knew that the chances that Craig would have identity problems in adulthood were extremely high.[4] I also knew that he was virtually certain to face strong homosexual temptations as a teen-ager and an adult if his condition could not be reversed to a normal male identity.

A Psychologist's Challenge

Craig obviously needed intensive help, his parents urgently wanted the best professional care available for him, and they were praying that God would help their son to be happy with a male identity and a male role so that he could grow with the possibility of being married and having children in later life. Even though there had never before been a proven psychological therapy that could be automatically applied to a case like this, I prayerfully accepted the challenge of developing a psychological treatment for Craig in the hope that with the cooperation of the parents, I could help Craig become normal.

At the same time, I realized that if we succeeded in Craig's case, the new psychological treatment might also be beneficial for hundreds of other children like Craig. Therefore, I set out from the beginning to document scientifically all the measurable aspects of Craig's problem. I conducted a clinical scientific study with the case of Craig to evaluate the impact of some new treatment procedures.[5]

As it turned out, the case of Craig provided the first scientific study demonstrating a successful treatment for severe feminine identity in a boy. The results of Craig's treatment and that of other boys provided one section of my dissertation at UCLA.[6] How then did we help Craig? And what is he like now as a teen-ager?

4. G. A. Rekers et al., "Child gender disturbances: A clinical rationale for intervention," *Psychotherapy: Theory, Research, and Practice* 14 (1977): 2 — 11.

5. G. A Rekers and O. I. Lovaas, "Behavioral treatment of deviant sex-role behaviors in a male child," *Journal of Applied Behavior Analysis* 7 (1974): 173 — 190.

6. "Pathological sex-role development in boys: Behavioral treatment and assessment," 1972.

Helping Parents to Help Their Boy

The key to Craig's treatment involved both of his parents. Instead of taking a "play therapy" approach, where a child might be seen for one hour a week in a play session at a clinic, I knew that Craig's treatment would require a much more intensive program. For this reason, I invested my energy in training his parents to serve, in effect, as the psychological therapists for their own son. In this way, the boy could benefit from special assistance during many of his waking hours during the week, rather than just during a one-hour session in the university psychology clinic office.

As I explained in chapters 2 and 3, the mother and father of a boy make an important difference for him. In this pilot case, I was fortunate that a father was present in the home. In later research, I found that this was a relatively rare situation for a boy with a severe sexual-identity disorder.

My careful evaluation of Craig's family concluded that the father had a closer relationship with Craig's eight-year-old brother than with Craig. Because Craig was not interested in the typical boys' games that his brother participated in, his father felt less inclined to spend time with him. Instead, the father spent considerable time playing ball and roughhousing with Craig's brother. For this reason, Craig had an intensely close relationship with his mother and a quite remote relationship with his father.

This family situation meant that I needed to discover a way to encourage a more normal relationship between Craig and his mother and to develop a new and closer relationship between Craig and his father.

My first step was to carefully measure Craig's masculine and feminine play and his masculine and feminine talking. I did this in both the psychology clinic and his home. Using scientific baseline observation measures, I found that if Craig were given an opportunity to play with either boys' or girls' toys in the clinic he would consistently play with the girls' toys between 85 and 100 percent of the time. In fact, on the average he played with the girls' toys 98 percent of the time and only rarely explored the boys' toys. This pattern of feminine play persisted through a series of sixteen sessions, interspersed over a four-week period, in the clinic. This pattern was the same whether

Craig played alone in a playroom (as I observed from behind a one-way mirror) or whether he played when his mother was present in the room.

But strikingly, whenever Craig's father was in the playroom to watch him play, Craig played predominantly with the boys' toys, but he did so in a very mundane and unenthusiastic way. When he played with the girls' toys, while alone or with his mother in the room, he was animated, excited, and involved in his play. But when his father stepped into the room, he would switch quickly to playing with the boys' toys in a bored, monotonous, and repetitive way. This meant that Craig had little genuine interest in playing with the boys' toys.

I also wanted to get some accurate record of Craig's play at home. First, I made some visits to Craig's home (yes, some psychologists do make house calls). I found out that Craig's four most frequent and compulsive feminine behaviors at home were playing with dolls, using feminine gestures and mannerisms, playing with girls, and taking a female role in play.

Then I taught Craig's mother how to record these four feminine behaviors on a check list that I made for her. This form had four boxes after each behavior for each day. I asked her to observe Craig carefully for ten minutes at four specific times each day.

If Craig played with girls during that ten-minute period, his mother would put a check mark in the column indicating "Plays with Girls." If he played with female dolls, she would place a check mark for that ten-minute period in the column marked "Plays with Female Dolls." If Craig exhibited effeminate body movements, she would make a check mark for that ten-minute period in the column marked "Feminine Gestures." Similarly, if Craig impersonated or pretended to be a female (for example, an actress, a mother, a female teacher) while playing games such as "house" or "school," then his mother would make a check mark after it in the column which was marked "Female Role Play."

From time to time, I sent a clinical assistant to the home to take records at the same time as the mother did in order to make sure that the mother's records were reliable. We continued these records of the behavior in the clinic and at the home all during treatment to see what effect the treatment would have on Craig's sex-role behavior.

Learning New Mothering Skills

I worked closely with Craig's mother because he was likely to act feminine while he was with her but not while he was with his father. From behind the one-way mirror, I observed Craig play in the clinic playroom with his mother present. I noticed that his mother made facial expressions that indicated her extreme displeasure whenever Craig picked up feminine toys and played with them.

Son Controls Mom

Craig's mother would frown, shake her head, and sometimes say sharply, "No, Craig, don't play like a girl." But Craig continued merrily along, playing like a girl. He had a devilish little grin which betrayed a certain pleasure he experienced by annoying his mother. His mother would tell me, "I don't know why he keeps on playing like a girl. I don't know why he's pretending he's a girl, when I scold him for doing it and when he knows it upsets me."

Mom Controls Son

I told Craig's mother that I was concerned about Craig persisting in his feminine behavior in her presence. I suggested trying a new strategy. I asked the mother to ignore Craig's feminine actions and to pay attention to him only if he was playing with boys' toys.

I wanted Craig's mother to try this new strategy in the clinic playroom while I watched. I helped her out by having her wear a "bug-in-the-ear" device which looks like a hearing aid but is a miniature radio receiver. This device picked up my comments to her from a microphone in the observation room. This meant that Craig could not hear me talking to his mother, so I could give her instructions while Craig played in front of her.

I gave the mother a large *Look* magazine to hold in her lap. I told her that whenever Craig started to play with the girls' toys, she should pick up the magazine from her lap and put it in front of her face to read it. If Craig switched to playing with the boys' toys, I would quickly tell her that he was playing with the boys' toys, and I reminded her to put down the magazine and play with Craig. In this way, I taught the mother to smile, attend, and verbally reward Craig's masculine play and to ignore his play with the girls' toys.

In a matter of only minutes, Craig switched to predominantly masculine play in his mother's presence. After six or seven weeks of this strategy, Craig was playing like any normal boy with the masculine toys when he was in front of his mother or when he was alone in the clinic.

A New Deal

However, at the same time, the records that the mother was taking on Craig's play at home showed that he was still highly feminine at home. At first I asked the mother to try ignoring Craig's feminine behavior at home in the same way she was doing so effectively in the clinic. But she found that the home environment made living much more complicated.

Craig's mother did not have the same amount of control over her son's behavior at home. It was so much easier for her to concentrate single-mindedly on ignoring feminine behavior and paying attention to masculine behavior in the clinic. Also, at home, Craig could easily observe how disgusted she would get when he played with the girls' toys. She had no way to conceal this from him, and he still delighted in getting her upset this way at home.

Therefore, I needed a new approach for Craig's mother to use at home. The mother needed a more powerful approach to normalize Craig's sex-role behavior at home. I decided to try a token-reinforcement system. In this approach, a child can earn tokens for good behavior.

In this case, we used ordinary blue and red poker chips for the token system. The blue tokens served as positive rewards. They could be exchanged for things the child liked, including candies, treats, and rewarding activities such as watching a favorite television program. One of Craig's favorite activities was to get ice cream from the ice-cream truck when it came by the house. So we set up a certain number of tokens that he would need to have accumulated to trade for money to buy an ice-cream bar.

Truth or Consequences

At first, I simply wanted Craig to get used to the idea of the token system. There were certain activities that his mother and father expected of him at home, such as picking up his dirty clothes and putting them into a hamper. In the first phase of using the token system, Craig would get a token for performing these helpful, responsible behaviors.

A bit later, I added another condition, involving red tokens which were given for undesirable behavior. The red token served as immediate consequence for an undesired behavior. The red tokens were saved up and later were exchanged for one of three consequences: the mother or father could subtract one blue token earned for every red token received; each red token could be exchanged for a time-out consequence (for example, each red token could result in a lapse of five minutes of a rewarding activity such as watching television); a red token might result in a mild swat from the father.

The mother's daily schedule with her three children was hectic. But it was easy for her to use this token system. Whenever Craig disobeyed his mother, she would tell him that he had performed a bad behavior and would immediately take out one red token and place it on the kitchen counter. Craig could see the red and blue tokens accumulating, although he could not reach them himself. This was a quick and easy disciplinary measure for the mother to carry out. She did not need to interrupt her work except to add a red token to the stack.

Later, when she had more time, Craig's mother could carry out the rest of the strategy. She could sit down with Craig and show him that he was losing one blue token for every red token he had accumulated. She could enforce a time-out procedure if she so decided. Or she could tell the father about the red tokens when he came home. If the parents agreed, the boy would receive a spank for each red token accumulated.

Reality Training

Craig eventually got used to this new disciplinary system where he was held accountable for his behavior. I then advised the parents to extend the token system to one aspect of his sex-role behaviors at a time.

At first, I told Craig that I wanted his mother to give him a red token each time he played with female dolls. I explained that he was playing with these girls' dolls too much and that we wanted to help him learn to leave those dolls alone by having him receive red tokens for playing with female dolls. His play with dolls (which had been quite frequent up to that point) ceased entirely once I explained this to him. Craig did not play with dolls again during the next twenty-nine weeks that we left this consequence in effect.

Several weeks later, I told Craig that he would receive a red token each time his mother saw him display a feminine body gesture such as swaying his hips, using a limp wrist, or sitting effeminately. I sat down and explained these feminine behaviors to him thoroughly. During the first two weeks that this new consequence was in effect, Craig displayed fewer body gestures and by the third week he had ceased all body gestures altogether. We left this red token consequence in effect for the next eighteen weeks, and during that time Craig did not earn any more red tokens for feminine gestures because those body movements stopped altogether with this strategy. So Craig stopped getting his mother upset by using his superfeminine gestures.

Next I told Craig that we were concerned that he spent all his time playing with girls and avoiding boys altogether. I told him if he continued to play only with girls that he would get red tokens each day that he played only with the girls. He immediately stopped playing with girls only and he began to play with boys in the neighborhood.

By this point in the program, Craig had also ceased taking female roles in play.

Like Father, Like Son

I encouraged Craig's father to take Craig and his brother on weekend camp-outs and to a weekly "Indian Guide" club meeting. For the first time, Craig and his father learned to enjoy one another's company.

This made it natural and easy for me to encourage the father to play with Craig in a nonthreatening way. I advised the father to spend an equal amount of time playing with both of his boys. This also helped Craig feel better about his relationship with his dad.

Fortunately, Craig's father followed this advice. His father became the most immediate source for Craig's learning what masculinity is all about. By feeling better about his relationship with his father, Craig began feeling better about his own masculinity.

Ten months had transpired since the time I had begun working with this family, and by now, Craig was indistinguishable from any other boy in terms of his sex-role behaviors. He had begun kindergarten and his teacher reported that he behaved the same as other boys at school. Craig's parents and neighbors also reported that he was now playing with other boys in a way that appeared very different from the time when he first came to the clinic.

I also brought Craig back into the clinic and again watched him play from behind the one-way mirror while he was alone in the playroom. I had a tape recorder on while he was playing in the playroom. Craig walked up to the girls' and boys' toys, hesitated for a moment as he looked at all the toys, and then he spontaneously said, "These are girls' toys here and those are boys' toys [pointing]. I'm a boy, so I'm going to play with the boys' toys." Craig's mother, at the end of this ten months' treatment, reported that he now looked "more like a typical boy" because he was no longer fussy about color-coordinating his clothes and keeping his hair neat. Craig now always referred to himself as a boy and assumed male roles when he played.

Craig at Seven

Twenty-six months later, when Craig was seven years old, I did a follow-up psychological evaluation and found that he was still behaving as a boy and still had his new male identity. But I found that he was relatively less skilled in some desired masculine play skills than were some other boys his age. I therefore enlisted the cooperation of Craig's father in order to set up training sessions in playing ball. For several months, I sent the clinical assistant out to make weekly visits to Craig's home and work with Craig and his father in playing ball together.[7] This intensive training helped Craig develop the skill needed to succeed better with his male peer group.

Craig at Nine

Three and one-half years after his treatment had been terminated, I asked an independent clinical psychologist to interview the boy and family members and to administer a battery of psychological tests.[8] At this point, Craig was nine years old and I found, as the other psychologist had found, that he had a normal male sexual identity as well as a normal emotional, social, and academic adjustment. The psychologist attributed this to the effects of my therapy, which included the parents' learning skills in behavior management. These skills, in effect, extended the treatment program indefinitely on an informal basis in Craig's own environment.

Craig at Fifteen

Finally, when Craig was fifteen years old, I arranged for another clinical psychologist to do a follow-up evaluation of Craig's sexual

7. Rekers and Lovaas, "Behavioral treatment."

8. G. A. Rekers, "Sexual Problems: Behavior Modification," in *Handbook of Treatment of Mental Disorders in Childhood and Adolescence*, ed. Benjamin B. Wolman (Englewood Cliffs, NJ: Prentice-Hall, 1978), chapter 17.

identity and general psychological adjustment.[9] This psychologist reported that Craig was indistinguishable from any other normal teen-age boy. He reported that Craig was developing normal masculine roles, had a normal male identity, had normal aspirations for growing up to be married and have a family, and was well-adjusted as a teen-age boy in general.

Preventing Perversion

Craig was the first child I worked with in the ten-year psychological treatment research project that I launched at the UCLA Psychology Department. My purpose for this project was to identify children at high risk for homosexual temptation and other deviant sexual problems.[10] This project was the first comprehensive scientific study undertaken with a preventative strategy for the problem of homosexuality.

My purpose was to intervene early in children's lives to head off the first step toward a problem with homosexuality, transsexualism, or transvestism. Therefore, I evaluated boys with the high likelihood of becoming vulnerable to the temptation to homosexuality or other related deviant behavior. Psychological treatment was offered to the families to prevent the development of a homosexual orientation by first reducing the vulnerability to homosexual temptation.

Childhood Sex-role Disturbance

Research studies on the childhood indicators of male homosexuality have found a striking pattern of feminine role behaviors in many cases. Compared with adult heterosexuals, a majority of adult male homosexuals have a childhood history which included extensive playing with dolls, wearing girls' dresses, playing with cosmetics, using feminine gestures, behavior, and talking, stating a desire to be a girl, preferring girl playmates, playing with girls' toys, play-acting

9. I express my appreciation to Drs. Larry N. Ferguson and Alexander C. Rosen for their independent evaluations.

10. G. A. Rekers, "A priori values and research on homosexuality," *American Psychologist* 33 (1978): 510 – 512; G. A. Rekers, "Play Therapy with Cross-Gender Identified Children," in *Handbook of Play Therapy*, ed. Charles E. Shaeffer and Kevin J. O'Connor (New York: Wiley, 1982).

feminine roles, and avoiding masculine play activities.[11] What is not yet understood is the finding that by adulthood, large numbers of these feminine boys have grown up to be masculine-appearing men, with the exception of their sexual orientation toward other men.

The Temptations of Feminine Males

In any event, long-term studies have traced various groups of these feminine behaviors in boys to the development of male homosexuality or other sexual deviation.[12] The same feminine childhood is reported by many adult male homosexuals, transvestites, and transsexuals.[13]

Bernard Zuger reported a twenty-year clinical follow-up study of such sex-role disturbed boys who received no psychological treatment.[14] By the time these boys had reached their twenties, 63 percent were homosexual, 6 percent were transvestite, 6 percent were transsexual and only 12 percent heterosexual. Significantly, 25 percent were so unhappy that they had attempted suicide by the time they were in their twenties, and 6 percent had succeeded in committing suicide. The depression and suicidal urges are strong reminders of the abnormality of this condition.

Helping Children with Sex-role Disturbance

I have developed new clinical psychological assessment procedures to diagnose sexual-identity problems in boys, in order to detect the indicators associated with a high vulnerability to abnormal sexual temptations.[15] With funding from six major clinical research grants

11. See review by Rekers et al., "Child gender disturbance."

12. *Ibid.*

13. *Ibid.*

14. "Effeminate behavior present in boys from childhood: Ten additional years of follow-up," *Comprehensive Psychiatry* 19 (1978): 363 – 396.

15. Rekers, "Psychosexual and Gender Problems," in *Behavioral Assessment of Childhood Disorders*; G. A. Rekers and J. P. Rudy, "Differentiation of childhood body gestures," *Perceptual and Motor Skills* 46 (1978): 839 – 845; G. A. Rekers and S. L. Mead, "Human sex differences in carrying behaviors: A replication and extension," *Perceptual and Motor Skills* 48 (1979): 625 – 626; G. A. Rekers, J. A. Sanders, and C. C. Strauss, "Developmental differentiation of adolescent body gestures," *Journal of Genetic Psychology* 138, no. 1 (1981): 123 – 131; G. A. Rekers et al., "Differentiation of adolescent activity participation," *The Journal of Genetic Psychology*, in press; G. A. Rekers and A. P. Jurich, "Development of Problems of Puberty and Sex Roles in Adolescents," in *Handbook of Clinical Child Psychology*, ed. Eugene Walker and Michael C. Roberts (New York: Wiley, 1982).

from the National Institute of Mental Health, I also developed a set of psychological intervention techniques designed to bring the boy back to normal sexual-identification patterns.[16] As in the case of Craig, whenever possible, the parents of the boy were involved in the strategy to assist the youngster.

Symptoms in Boys

In conclusion, what are the symptoms that an alert parent can watch for? Here is a list of symptoms of sexual-identity disturbance in boys. Different boys might have a different combination of two or more of these behaviors persisting over twelve months' time:

dressing in feminine clothing

using cosmetics, such as lipstick

using feminine body gestures and gait

16. G. A. Rekers, "Therapies Dealing with the Child's Sexual Difficulties," in *Enfance et Sexualite/Childhood and Sexuality*, ed. Jean-Marc Samson (Montreal and Paris: Les Editions Etudes Vivantes, 1980); G. A. Rekers, "Play Therapy with Cross-Gender Identified Boys," in *Handbook of Play Therapy*; G. A. Rekers, O. I. Lovaas, and B. P. Low, "The behavioral treatment of a 'transsexual' preadolescent boy," *Journal of Abnormal Child Psychology* 2 (1974): 99 – 116, reprinted (digest) in *Therapies for School Behavior Problems*, ed. Howard L. Millman, Charles E. Shaeffer, and Jeffrey Cohen (San Francisco: Jossey-Bass, 1980), pp. 305 – 307; G. A. Rekers et al., "Childhood gender identity change: Operant control over sex-typed play and mannerisms," *Journal of Behavior Therapy and Experimental Psychiatry* 7 (1976): 51 – 57; G. A. Rekers and J. W. Varni, "Self-monitoring and self-reinforcement processes in a pre-transsexual boy," *Behavior Research and Therapy* 15 (1977): 177 – 180; G. A. Rekers and J. W. Varni, "Self-regulation of gender-role behaviors: A case study," *Journal of Behavior Therapy and Experimental Psychiatry* 8 (1977): 427 – 432; G. A. Rekers et al., "Assessment of childhood gender behavior change," *Journal of Child Psychology and Psychiatry* 18 (1977): 53 – 65; L. N. Ferguson and G. A. Rekers, "Non-aversive intervention for public childhood masturbation," *The Journal of Sex Research* 15, no. 3 (1979): 213 – 223, reprinted (digest) in *Therapies for School Behavior Problems*, pp. 365 – 367; G. A. Rekers, "Sex-role behavior change: Intrasubject studies of boyhood gender disturbance," *The Journal of Psychology* 103 (1979): 255 – 269; G. A. Rekers, "Assessment and treatment of childhood gender problems," in *Advances in Clinical Child Psychology*, ed. Benjamin B. Lahey and Alan E. Kazdin (New York: Plenum, 1977), volume 1, chapter 7; G. A. Rekers and G. C. Milner, "Sexual identity disorders in childhood and adolescence," *Journal of the Florida Medical Association* 65 (1975): 962 – 964; G. A. Rekers and G. C. Milner, "How to diagnose and manage childhood sexual disorders," *Behavioral Medicine* 6, no. 4 (1979): 18 – 21; G. A. Rekers, "Childhood sexual identity disorders," *Medical Aspects of Human Sexuality* 15, no. 3 (1981): 141 – 142; G. A. Rekers and G. C. Milner, "Early detection of sexual identity disorders," *Medical Aspects of Human Sexuality* 15, no. 11 (1981): 32EE – 32FF.

being preoccupied with girls' toys and activities and avoiding boys' toys and activities

preferring play with girls instead of play with boys

talking with a high femininelike voice and/or talking predominantly about feminine topics instead of masculine ones

taking a female role in play consistently

masturbating, with women's undergarments or clothing as a stimulus

stating a desire to be a girl, or to grow up to bear infants or breast-feed babies

asking to have his penis removed

If several of these behaviors persist in a child, even as young as four years, for more than twelve months, a sexual-identity problem might be developing.

9

Correcting Sexual-identity Problems in Girls

Sexual-identity problems are more rare in girls than they are in boys. No one knows for certain why this is the case. It might be due to the fact that in earliest childhood (the first five years of life) approximately 11 percent of all boys grow up in a fatherless home while fewer than 1 percent of all girls grow up in a motherless home.[1] Therefore girls may be more likely to have an adequate female role model to identify with in younger childhood than boys are likely to have a male role to identify with in younger childhood. On the other hand, there may be more boys with sex-role difficulties because of some cultural influence, such as the observation that in Northern European and Northern American countries there is a greater rigidity in masculine role stereotypes than there is for feminine role stereotypes.[2]

Nevertheless, girls sometimes experience problems with normal sexual identification. These girls have childhoods that are similar, in most cases, to those reported by adult female homosexuals and transsexuals.[3] For this reason, it is particularly important to detect sexual-identity problems in girls in order to possibly prevent homosexual temptations for these girls in later adolescence and adulthood.

1. U.S. Bureau of the Census, *Statistical Abstracts of the United States: 1978* (Washington, DC: U.S. Department of Commerce, 1978).
2. G.A. Rekers et al., "Sex-role stereotypy and professional intervention for childhood gender disturbances," *Professional Psychology* 9 (1978): 127 – 136.
3. G.A. Rekers and S.L. Mead, "Female sex-role deviance: Early identification and developmental intervention," *Journal of Clinical Child Psychology* 9, no. 3 (1980): 199 – 203.

What Ever Happened with Becky?

Do you remember Becky from chapter 2? Becky was the seven-year, eleven-month-old girl with two younger sisters. Her parents were divorced. Briefly, Becky had a long history of rejecting feminine clothing and a feminine role, while expressing the desire to be a boy, preferring to appear in boys' clothing, and using boys' body gestures. I had determined by a complete psychological evaluation that Becky was very likely to experience deviant sexual temptations in later life because of her male sexual identity.[4]

Father Absent and Mother Unavailable

Becky's mother was very interested in obtaining psychological help for her daughter, but she was not available for extensive partici-pation in a treatment program herself because her infant daughter had a life-threatening health condition which meant that the young-est daughter might not survive past early childhood. Because the mother was the only parent in the home, the special care of this infant daughter was very demanding and made it difficult for her to participate in a treatment program for Becky. For this reason, I needed to develop a therapy program which could be carried out primarily in the clinic, rather than training the mother in more complicated procedures to carry out in the home.

Revealing Child's Play

Becky was given the opportunity to play with two different sets of masculine and feminine toys in the clinic playroom while I observed her from behind a one-way mirror. I observed Becky play in the room alone as well as with various noninteracting adults. I found that Becky played predominantly with the boys' toys and that she was not consistently feminine in her play while alone, or with a female stranger, a male stranger, or her mother present in the room.

Self-help

Therefore, my assistant and I brought in yet another set of boys' and girls' toys and taught Becky a self-monitoring technique using

4. G. A. Rekers and S. L. Mead, "Early intervention for female sexual identity disturbance: Self-monitoring of play behavior," *Journal of Abnormal Child Psychology* 7, no. 4 (1979): 405 – 423.

a wrist counter. This wrist counter is a simple device that golf players use to keep score. We gave her a wrist counter and told her, "You may play with any of the toys you like, but you may only press the wrist counter when you are playing with girls' toys." Then we pointed to each toy and labeled each one as a girl's toy or a boy's toy.

We also let Becky wear the "bug-in-the-ear" device so that we could talk to her from the observation room. We reminded Becky that she could press the wrist counter while she was playing with the girls' toys. After a while, we stopped reminding her and she was able to give herself points for playing with girls' toys. The therapy sessions using this approach changed her play from predominantly masculine to high rates of feminine play with the girls' toys.

Meanwhile ... at Home

I sent a female clinical assistant to Becky's home to take an inventory of Becky's toys at home and to make a list of every toy (whether it was masculine, feminine, or neutral). We found that she had only a few feminine toys but a large number of masculine toys at home.

In home visits, the assistant had Becky again wear the wrist counter while playing with the toys in her room. This gave Becky some experience in playing appropriately with the girls' toys at home. After a few sessions, Becky complained that she was tired of her girls' toys and began playing with boys' toys in her room.

Therefore, I decided to allow Becky to buy some new girls' toys. The assistant told Becky, "Since you've been so good playing with girls' toys, we're going to buy you some more girls' toys as a reward." Then several female assistants took Becky to a toy store. They served as examples for her by saying, "When I was a girl, I used to play with this," while they pointed out various girls' toys in the store. Becky chose a doll, a doll's hair-grooming set, a plastic purse, and a jump rope to buy at the store. Then the assistants continued the training procedure, encouraging Becky to play with the girls' toys at home.

Who Am I?

In the early phases of this treatment, Becky told the assistant that she wished she were a boy and that she hoped she would never have a baby when she grew up. Another time she said, "I look ugly in dresses. I get sick in dresses 'cuz I like to play with boys."

But as therapy progressed and Becky obtained more and more

rewarding experience in playing with girls' toys, she began to take on more female identity. Earlier in therapy she said, "I'm getting this stuff [perfume] off of me, and I ain't kidding. I better not smell like a girl." But after she had more experience in playing with girls' toys, she asked the assistant, "Where's the make-up? You should have gotten the make-up here. Doesn't a lady wear make-up?"

After a few months of these therapy sessions, the assistant asked Becky if she would rather be a boy than a girl and Becky replied, "No, because boys can't have babies and because if you get a divorce, the woman gets to keep the baby." At this point in therapy, Becky began wearing jewelry and perfume at home on her own. She started to become interested in the boys at school as potential "boyfriends." Her mother said that this had never happened before.

Becky's mother was asked to praise her whenever she saw Becky playing with feminine toys at home. She also was asked to praise Becky for wearing girls' clothes and for taking girls' roles.

With these improvements, Becky also ceased her deviant sexual activity that was present earlier before treatment.

Accepting Femininity

After these treatment procedures were completed, I had an independent clinical psychologist reevaluate Becky with a comprehensive set of psychological tests.[5] She scored high in femininity as opposed to masculinity in this posttreatment testing. At one point, when Becky was asked which pair of shoes a neutral figure would like to play dress-up with, Becky chose the high-heeled shoes and said, " 'Cuz I'm a girl, ain't I?" as if her response should have been obvious to the psychologist.

Four-and-one-half months after the completion of her six months' treatment, I arranged for another evaluation by another independent clinical psychologist. In each instance, when Becky was given an opportunity to play with masculine or feminine sex-typed toys, she played 100 percent of the time with feminine or girls' toys. Following an extensive battery of clinical psychology tests, a male examiner and a female observer were both asked to determine if Becky had a sex-role disturbance. Both judged her to have a normal sexual iden-

5. *Ibid.*

tity at the follow-up time. This means that the effects of the treatment appeared to be stable and to hold up over time.[6]

Right and Wrong Sex Roles

These approaches to encourage Becky to act like a girl resulted not only in her acting more and more like a girl, but also in her feeling more and more like a girl, as evidenced by the things that she said. This is an important aspect of my research findings with the children—that is, if we can encourage the child to act like a boy if he is a boy or to act like a girl if she is a girl, then this child will gradually take on the correct sexual identity.

As the children gain experience in the correct sex-role behaviors, they become more and more normal in their identification with their anatomy and their appropriate sex role. Homosexual behavior is really an example of wrong sex-role behavior. For example, for a female to have sex with another female is a very "masculine" thing to do. On the other hand, for a male to have sexual relations with another male is a very "feminine" thing to do. Therefore it is very important for the young child to learn how to take on the appropriate sex role in all areas of life in order to identify properly with his or her own sex at an early age.

Alert and dedicated parents can use their influence effectively to help their little boys act and feel like boys. Similarly, mothers and fathers have a strong influence in helping their daughters to behave femininely and to feel comfortable about being a girl. The examples of Craig and Becky illustrate how extreme a child's confusion about sexual identity can be. My summaries on helping this boy and this girl clearly teach this fact: If we encourage a boy to behave in a masculine way, he will feel like a boy. And if we encourage a girl to behave in a feminine way, she will adapt to being a girl.

Symptoms in Girls

It is true that sexual-identity problems are more common in boys than in girls. This might be because sexual deviations occur more frequently in men than women as a rule, and because American

6. *Ibid.*

society is more concerned about feminine behavior in a boy than it is concerned about masculine behavior in a girl. Nevertheless, sexual-identity disturbances have been reported in girls.[7]

In conclusion, here is a list of possible symptoms of girlhood sexual-identity problems:

repeatedly refusing to wear girls' clothing, jewelry, or cosmetics

using masculine gestures and gait

rigidly insisting on appearing like "one of the boys"

avoiding play opportunities with other girls and playing primarily with the boys, like "one of the boys"

projecting her voice to a masculinelike tone and/or predominantly talking about male activities

expressing a desire to be called by a boy's name or nickname

masturbating, with men's clothing as a stimulus

expressing a desire to have a penis

asking for a sex-change procedure, such as breast removal, or male hormones

If a number of these behaviors persist over many months, a concerned parent might well have his or her daughter professionally tested to screen for a possible sex-role disturbance.

---

7. Rekers and Mead, "Early intervention"; "Female sex-role deviance."

10

Rearing Masculine Boys and Feminine Girls

I have devoted nine chapters to presenting considerable detail about two key influences that parents have in shaping their children's sexual identities.

First, parents shape normal sexual identities in their sons and daughters by properly contributing the distinctive roles of father and mother to their family life.

Second, parents shape normal sexual identities in their children by encouraging their sons to behave in masculine ways and by encouraging their daughters to behave in feminine ways.

Let's summarize each of these two key influences in a way that will be easy to remember.

The First Key: Properly Contributing Distinctive Roles

Chapters 1-5 were devoted to this principle.

The Unisex Myth

Chapter 1 exposed the unisex myth which tries to undermine the distinction between fathers' and mothers' roles. While the evil excesses of the menacing macho myth and male chauvinism are to be recognized, they should not lead us to the opposite and equally unreasonable evils of radical feminism and the unisex mentality. We should *not* end all distinctions based on sex just because that distinction has been abused by some men in the past and present.

Sexual-identity Problems

In chapter 2, I used the examples of a boy and a girl to illustrate what confusion and suffering occurs when children are not reared properly in male and female roles. The families of these disturbed children were examined, and it was discovered that the parents *failed* to properly contribute both the distinctive father role and the distinctive mother role for their children.

Fathers' and Mothers' Roles

In chapter 3, I emphasized that if a child is to grow up with the potential for adjusting easily to a normal heterosexual marriage and family life, that child must learn the appropriate sex role while growing up. This means that little boys need to identify with their father or with a father substitute who serves as a role model for him. An affectionate and pleasant relationship with a father helps the boy learn to feel comfortable with his own masculinity. If a little boy has an affectionate and nurturing father to identify with, the boy will learn what it means to be a male. And if the little boy has a warm, affectionate, and nurturant relationship with the father figure, the boy will feel good about the father's masculinity. Eventually these good feelings about his father's masculinity will be translated into good feelings about his own masculinity.

In the same way, if a little girl has a warm and nurturant relationship with her mother, she will learn from the mother how to behave in a feminine way. She will also feel good about her mother's femininity. Feeling good about her mother's femininity will gradually translate into good feelings about her own femininity.

When the father (not the mother) leads the family, the sexual identities of both the sons and daughters are promoted in a normal way.

The Folly of a Unisex Parent

In chapters 4 and 5, I emphasized the importance of parents properly contributing distinctive father and mother roles. We saw how a unisex mother followed radical feminist principles, only to find that she destroyed her family and lost legal custody of her three pre-school-age daughters. From her example, we observed how the unisex mentality undermines the nuclear family by leading parents into bisexual escapades, all under the banner that advocates "an end to all distinctions based on sex." The alarming feminist ideas result in family disintegration. Karla's life of unstable sexual affairs with an ever-changing set of male and female partners conformed with the unisex myth perpetuated by feminists and humanists. But Karla failed to contribute the proper mother role for her daughters' welfare. Her openly-acknowledged bisexual conduct threatens the future sexual-identity development of her daughters.

The Straight Truth

Discarding the unisex myth as extremist, simplistic, and destructive to family life, my review of child-development research and Scripture confirmed the first key to shaping normal sexual identity in children—namely, the parents' proper contribution of the distinctive *father* and *mother* roles to their family life.

The Second Key: Encouraging Masculinity in Boys and Femininity in Girls

Chapters 6 – 9 were devoted to this principle that parents need to shape specific masculine behaviors in boys and specific feminine behaviors in girls.

What Are Little Boys and Girls Made Of?

Chapters 6 and 7 reviewed the reasons why, in younger childhood, little boys need to learn how to behave like boys and little girls need to learn how to behave like girls. As the little boy learns how to behave as a boy, for example, by taking the role of "daddy" when he plays, then he not only will master what it means to be a male, but he also will see himself behaving like a male, which will solidify or reinforce his identity as a male. By the same token, the little girl who is encouraged to act in a feminine way will feel more and more feminine as she grows up.

This is why my treatment for children with sexual-identity problems, reviewed in chapters 8 and 9, has involved procedures to get the child to behave in a sex-appropriate way.[1] I have developed pro-

1. G. A. Rekers, "Assessment and Treatment of Childhood Gender Problems," in *Advances in Clinical Child Psychology,* ed. Benjamin B. Lahey and Alan E. Kazdin (New York: Plenum, 1977), volume 1, chapter 7.

grams to help the little boy gain experience in acting like a boy. With this practice, the child learns to have a normal sexual identity.

Sex-role behavior and sexual identity have certain connections:

The boy who is encouraged to act in a masculine way will develop a firm male identity.

The boy who develops a firm male identity will behave in a more masculine way.

Similarly, the girl who is encouraged to act in a feminine way will develop a firm female identity.

The girl who develops a firm female identity will behave in a more feminine way.

This means that parents need to be attentive to the proper sex-role behaviors for males and females, and carefully teach these behaviors to their children.

What Are Masculinity and Femininity?

The meaning of sexual identity cannot be understood from the perspective of the unisex mentality, because that viewpoint insists upon "an end to all distinctions based on sex." But similarly, the full essence of sexual identity cannot be understood from the perspective of modern scholarship, which fragments reality into the narrow and separate specialties of biology, psychology, sociology, and theology. Modern universities no longer seek for an integrative meaning of the *whole* person. Instead, scholarship is so departmentalized that our institutions of higher education should be renamed "diversities" instead of "universities." When studying human sexual identity, modern researchers are largely content with subdividing the subject into more and more manageable fragments. The professors become specialized experts who, according to a popular saying, seek to "learn more and more about less and less, until they know everything there is to know about nothing."

Unfortunately, therefore, contemporary "experts" on sexual identity have pursued the subject from the narrow perspective of just psychology or only sociology, for example. These modern minds disregard the relationship of sexual identity to the whole person and to the whole of truth. In this fashion, the questions of ultimate moral responsibility, the spiritual dimension, and meaning and value can all be blithely ignored. While such "experts" insist that their studied fragment still has some relative meaning, the essence of full maleness or femaleness is actually lost. For example, one psychologist labeled men with the largest number of extramarital affairs as "more heterosexual" than those men who had remained faithful to one wife. That psychologist had reduced the topic of human sexuality to a narrow area and divested himself of any responsibility to study and honor the larger concept. The myopia of dividing truth into subspecialties can obscure the truth altogether!

True Masculinity

The popular *Playboy* platitudes of our generation falsely preach the notion that the most masculine attribute is unrestrained intercourse. This irresponsible attitude pretends that we can isolate biological masculinity from social or moral aspects of the male role. But genuine masculinity acknowledges the interconnecting biological, psychological, social, and spiritual responsibilities attending the male role in all full sexual expression. Therefore, promiscuous sexual acts outside the protective confines of permanent marriage are really counterfeit masculinity. *Playboy's* image of masculinity is pseudomasculinity because it is not socially and morally responsible masculinity.

The sexual identity of a boy or man rests upon much more than his genital functions. There are social and moral as well as physical attributes that define a man as a man. The male role has been understood throughout history as embodying much more than the male reproductive act. As a whole person, the man's role involves social responsibilities of father and husband which accompany the act of sexual intercourse. As a whole person, the man's spiritual responsibilities as moral leader and provider attend the procreative sexual act. Marital fidelity and collaborative responsibility for children are intrinsic to the true and complete masculine role.

We cannot understand the essence of masculinity or the fullness of male sexual identity if we separate the different aspects of being a man. Instead, we need to consider the physical, psychological, social, and spiritual dimensions of the male role together. If we take all of these aspects into account, then we have answers for these questions:

Can a man be fully masculine without fathering a child? Yes.

Can a man be fully masculine without marrying a woman? Yes.

At the same time, this wholistic perspective teaches us that a man who promiscuously pursues heterosexual intercourse outside of marriage is diminishing his masculinity. And a male who engages in homosexual acts is also abandoning true masculinity.

Scripture's teaching clearly prescribes a moral dimension to the male role:

It is good for a man not to marry. But since there is so much immorality, each man should have his own wife. . . . [I Cor. 7:1b — 2a]

If anyone does not provide for his relatives, and especially for his immediate family, he has denied the faith and is worse than an unbeliever. [I Tim. 5:8]

Similarly, encourage the young men to be self-controlled. In everything set them an example by doing what is good. [Titus 2:6 — 7a]

Men are to take a lead in prayer in worship services, and they are instructed to avoid the pitfalls of anger and competitive strife: "I want men everywhere to lift up holy hands in prayer, without anger or disputing" (I Tim. 2:8).

The proper male role involves treating "older women as mothers, and younger women as sisters, with absolute purity" (I Tim. 5:2).

The moral dimension should never be left out of any discussion of proper male sexual identity and proper masculine roles. This fact is apparent in this biblical passage:

I write to you, fathers, because you have known him who is from the beginning.

I write to you, young men, because you have overcome the evil one.

I write to you, dear children, because you have known the Father.

I write to you, fathers, because you have known him who is from the beginning.

I write to you, young men, because you are strong, and the word of God lives in you, and you have overcome the evil one.

Do not love the world or anything in the world. If anyone loves the world, the love of the Father is not in him. For everything in the

world—the cravings of sinful man, the lust of his eyes and the boast-
ing of what he has and does—comes not from the Father but from
the world. The world and its desires pass away, but the man who
does the will of God lives forever. [I John 2:13 – 17]

True Femininity

Similarly, a true female sexual identity involves the whole person
in her biological, psychological, social, and spiritual life:

It is true femininity to experience sexual intimacy in the protective
confines of marriage with one's husband, but extramarital promiscuity of the *Playboy*-bunny image is pseudofemininity.

It is true femininity to conceive and bear a child in marriage, but
it is unfeminine to expose oneself to pregnancy out of wedlock.

It is true femininity and motherhood to protect the unborn child
from outside harm from tobacco or alcohol use, but it is unfeminine and contrary to true motherhood to deliberately abort a
child.

Scripture clearly defines the feminine role in terms of its biological,
social, and moral dimensions taken together:

So I counsel younger widows to marry, to have children, to manage their homes and to give the enemy no opportunity for slander.
[I Tim. 5:14]

Likewise, teach the older women to be reverent in the way they live,
not to be slanderers or addicted to much wine, but to teach what
is good. Then they can train the younger women to love their husbands and children, to be self-controlled and pure, to be busy at
home, to be kind, and to be subject to their husbands, so that no
one will malign the word of God. [Titus 2:3 – 5]

So the New Testament description of domestic responsibility is
the promotion of love, kindness, and sensible purity—not performing "women's work."

A woman should learn in quietness and full submission. I do not
permit a woman to teach or to have authority over a man; she must
be silent. [I Tim. 2:11 – 12]

Both I Corinthians 11 and Ephesians 5 ascribe to the woman the role of a model believer. It is only in the church and the home where women are commanded by Scripture to be uniquely submissive to men. So this submissive role does not apply to places of employment, in government, or in any other social place. "As submission in the church and the home is observed, we are reminded of our duty to be subject to Christ since the woman is a perfect picture of a believer ('the glory of man,' I Cor. 11:7). Admittedly, this is a 'great mystery'; nevertheless, we can all be instructed by it."[2]

In our twentieth-century culture, permeated as it is by Madison Avenue advertising, we might easily fall prey to the idea that a female identity is bolstered by the latest cosmetic wonders and the finest in feminine attire. This is a culturally-conditioned definition of femininity.

I also want women to dress modestly, with decency and propriety, not with braided hair or gold or pearls or expensive clothes, but with good deeds, appropriate for women who profess to worship God. [I Tim. 2:9 – 10]

Of course, this is not to say that girls should be prohibited from using modest amounts of cosmetics. But the point is that true femininity is an inner quality and not mere outward adornment. In fact, overemphasis upon outward appearance can actually detract from true femininity.

Distinctions in Male and Female Identity

Now that the reader has thoughtfully considered nine-and-one-half chapters that are devoted to many important aspects of shaping the sexual identity of a child, a summary table (see Table 1) can be offered with minimal risk that it will be viewed in a simplistic or superficial way. I hope that studying this table will help to put everything I have discussed in perspective. And I hope the issues of all the previous chapters will come to mind and help flesh out this table.

Contrary to the unisex myth, there *are* distinctions between male

2. See Michael Braun and George Alan Rekers, *The Christian in an Age of Sexual Eclipse* (Wheaton, IL: Tyndale, 1981), p. 157. See also chapters 4, 5, and 7.

and female roles. Some of these distinctions are absolute differences, based upon biological and moral realities. Other distinctions between the masculine and the feminine are culturally-based.

Biologically-defined Sex Roles

Notice that each box in the figure is numbered in the upper left-hand corner. Look now at box 1 and box 2.

Box 1 gives examples of feminine sex roles which are *absolutely* feminine because they are based upon the unique biology and anatomy of the female. For example, little girls learn to imitate a mother's role, which includes fantasizing or play-acting about growing up, being married, getting pregnant, delivering a baby, and breast-feeding the little one. Parents should encourage and approve their little girl's play-acting of this feminine role. It helps the girl develop a normal female identity.

Box 2 gives examples of masculine sex roles which are *absolutely* masculine because they are based upon the unique biology and anatomy of the male.[3] It is important, for example, for the boy to learn that he will *not* grow up with the biological possibility of having sexual intercourse with a man, getting pregnant, delivering a baby, or breast-feeding the infant. This is essential in order to shape a normal male identity in the boy. While the boy should be encouraged

3. There are also gender-linked differences in abilities and in physical and psychological traits which are not discussed here in length. The most obvious biological differences are that gestation, lactation, and menstruation occur in females only, and sperm production in the male only. Numerous research studies have also found that males, as a group, tend to score higher in measures of physical strength and fleetness (related to sex differences in muscles), certain mathematical skills, visual-spatial skills, and in gross-muscle movements. On the other hand, females tend to score higher, as a group, in measures of certain verbal skills, resistance to certain illnesses and disease, tactile sensitivity, and fine-muscle movements involved in manual dexterity. In the area of psychological traits, boys as a group are more aggressive, on average, than girls, and boys are more active in boisterous play than girls. On the other hand, girls score higher, as a group, on measures of nurturance, sociability, and empathy. The research studies demonstrating these sex differences are reviewed by several recent reports, including Eleanor E. Maccoby and Carol N. Jacklin, *The Psychology of Sex Differences* (Stanford, CA: Stanford University Press, 1974); Diane McGuinness and Karl H. Pribram, "The Origins of Sensory Bias in the Development of Gender Differences in Perception and Cognition," in *Cognitive Growth and Development— Essays in Honor of Herbert G. Birch*, ed. by Morton Bortner (New York: Brunner/Mazel, 1978); John Money and Anke A. Ehrhardt, *Man and Woman, Boy and Girl: The Differentiation and Dimorphism of Gender Identity from Conception to Maturity* (Baltimore: Johns Hopkins, 1972); C. Hutt, "Biological bases of psychological sex differences," *American Journal of Diseases in Childhood* 132 (1978): 170 – 177.

Table 1

Examples of Sex-role Distinctions

		Feminine Sex Role	Masculine Sex Role
Absolute Sex-role Distinctions	**Biologically Defined**	**1** Breast-feeding an infant Delivering a baby Being a mother	**2** Impregnating a female by sexual intercourse Being a father
	Morally Defined Based upon Sex Differences	**3** Modest clothing of upper torso Abstaining from actions during pregnancy that would endanger the life of the child (such as abstaining from alcohol or illicit drug intake and from deliberate abortion) Abstaining from sexual relations with females Being submissive to husband's leadership at home	**4** Financially supporting one's children Abstaining from sexual relations with males Abstaining from sexual relations outside the protective confines of marriage Providing moral and spiritual leadership in the home

Culturally-based Sex-role Distinctions

Culturally Defined Based upon Biological Sex Differences	**5** Using the women's room Wearing a dress Singing in a female choir Living in a sorority	**6** Grooming a beard Shaving the facial hair Playing professional sports on all-male teams Using the men's room Serving in combat Singing in a male quartet Living in a fraternity
Culturally Defined Based upon Arbitrary But Legitimate (Benign) Assignment	**7** Wearing lipstick Wearing fingernail polish Wearing mascara Shaving underarms or legs Carrying a purse	**8** Wearing a suit and necktie Having a man's haircut Opening doors for women and girls Paying for a date with a woman
Culturally Defined Based upon Arbitrary and Harmful Stereotypes Which Should Be Abolished	**9** Nurse Airline cabin attendant Secretary Lower pay for same job done by a man	**10** Doctor Airline pilot President Higher pay for same job done by a woman Male chauvinism Macho male stereotypes Sexual harassment of women Lewd jokes, locker-room language

to be nurturant, sensitive, and caring for infants (in preparation for fulfilling the commands to fathers in Ephesians 6:4, Colossians 3:21, and I Timothy 5:8, for example), it is important to teach the boy that he cannot grow up to marry a man or to be a woman himself.

Morally-defined Sex Roles

Box 3 gives some examples of feminine sex roles which are *absolutely* feminine because they are based upon unique moral responsibilities of women, as set forth in Scripture. Modest clothing of the upper torso should be taught to girls, and not boys, to train them to fulfill the moral teaching of I Timothy 2:9 — 10, for example. When parents emphasize this reason for having the girl dress differently than the boy, it reinforces her separate and distinct female identity. Protecting and preserving the life of the unborn child is a feminine responsibility taught by Scripture[4] and should be taught to every girl by her parents. The shaping of the girl's sexual identity also involves teaching her that women cannot select other women as sexual partners. In childhood and the teen-age years, the girl's mother should teach her daughter, by word and example, how to fulfill the uniquely feminine role of submissiveness in the home and the church. Of course, this moral distinction for the female role does not extend outside the church and home. The domestic responsibilities of the woman, as biblically defined (for example, I Tim. 5:8 — 14; Titus 2:3 — 5) are also morally-based aspects of the female role.

Box 4 provides examples of absolute masculine distinctives which are based upon unique moral responsibilities of men, as set forth in the Bible. Fathers, in particular, should teach these truths to their sons by word and example. The male role includes providing spiritual leadership in the home and church, as well as supporting his wife and children in family life. The moral standards for sexual conduct teach that true masculinity enters into sexual union only within the protective and loving confines of marriage. Premarital and extra-

---

4. Compare the theological truths in Genesis 1:27 — 28; 3:16; Exodus 20:14; 21:22 — 25; Psalm 22:9 — 10; Philippians 2:3 — 4; Titus 2:3 — 5; and I Timothy 5:14. The feminine responsibility for protecting and preserving the life of the unborn child is discussed in more detail by Clifford E. Bajema, *Abortion and the Meaning of Personhood* (Grand Rapids: Baker, 1974); Braun and Rekers, *The Christian in an Age of Sexual Eclipse*; Harold O. J. Brown, *Death before Birth* (New York: Thomas Nelson, 1977); Francis A. Schaeffer and C. Everett Koop, *Whatever Happened to the Human Race?* (Old Tappan, NJ: Revell, 1979). See also the article by Harold O. J. Brown, "Abortion and Child Abuse," *Christianity Today,* October 7, 1977, p. 34.

marital sexual intimacies are decidedly unmasculine and undermine the development of a confident and secure male identity. Similarly, boys should be taught that sexual relations with other males are not only wrong but are a symptom as well as a cause of a confused sexual identity. A male who has sex with another male calls his own masculinity into serious doubt. True masculinity reserves sexual acts for marriage, where the full moral, social, and biological responsibilities of manhood can be fulfilled as intended by the Creator.

Culturally-defined Sex Roles

There are three different kinds of culturally-based sex-role distinctions. Because these distinctions are not *absolutes*, it is essential that parents notice the real differences between these.

Culturally-defined, with Biological Basis

These male and female roles have come about by an interaction of cultural and biological factors. Society has taken note of certain differences in the anatomy of males and females and has then made some cultural assignments based on those differences.

Look at boxes 5 and 6 in the table. These are simply examples of many ways that males and females do different things in our society, because of their sex. It is important that you teach these differences to your children so they will get along well in everyday life. People in our culture expect different things from males than they do of females. To fit into society, your child needs to learn these things. But another benefit of teaching these distinctions to children is that they help boys feel like boys and girls feel like girls. It would be damaging to children's sexual-identity development if we parents failed to point out these sex differences to children in everyday life.

Consider some of these examples. Girls are taught to use the women's room and boys to use the men's room. Men either shave their beard or grow it out and groom it. Girls wear dresses and training bras. Boys and girls are placed on separate athletic teams which take into account their different rates of physical maturation and strength.

Culturally-defined, with Arbitrary But Legitimate Assignment

Every culture has a different set of behaviors which are arbitrarily classified as masculine or feminine (see boxes 7 and 8). Now, there is nothing wrong with this if these arbitrary categories do not interfere with the freedom of individuals of both sexes to develop their potential competencies. As long as the arbitrary social labels of "for men only" or "for women only" do not hinder freedom to use one's talents, then they are benign or harmless sex-role stereotypes.

For example, in our culture, women may wear lipstick, fingernail polish, and mascara, as well as shave their underarms and legs. These things, along with wearing dresses and sometimes wearing their hair differently, all serve to highlight the differences between males and females. In the same way, men and boys often have their hair cut in a recognizable male fashion and they sometimes wear clothing, such as a suit and necktie, that is distinctively worn more by men than women.

There are also various social roles and rules of etiquette which distinguish males from females. For example, men and boys often hold doors open for women and girls and let them walk in first. Men, in North American society at least, tend to shake hands more than women do, and women tend to hug one another more than men do to one another.

All these kinds of male and female differences are largely culturally-based with little or no connection to the biological differences between man and women. So a parent might ask, "Should I teach these kinds of arbitrary cultural distinctions to my children?"

The answer should be yes for most examples of benign cultural sex-role stereotypes. There are two reasons for this. First, if your child will be living for years in this culture, he or she will get along better with peers and with society in general if these sex-role distinctions are learned. Boys, for example, might suffer severe ridicule and social rejection if they regularly appeared with lipstick, mascara, and bright red fingernail polish on. A youth who asks a girl out for a dinner date might be socially embarrassed—and the girl unprepared—if the young man did not realize the social expectation is that the male pays for the female's dinner if he invited her out. Social and psychological adjustment depend upon teaching the young person these sex-role stereotypes.

The second reason for parents teaching these arbitrary sex-role stereotypes to their children is that such stereotypes help boys develop male identities and girls develop female identities. In childhood and adolescence, the boy and girl do not have the opportunity to experience many of the *absolute* sex-role distinctions. For instance, the girl cannot base her female identity on daily breast-feeding of infants, because she must await marriage in adulthood for that. But she can feel quite feminine and different from boys by carrying a purse or putting on nail polish on a day-to-day basis. Little boys can feel "just like daddy" when they wear a little suit and tie.

In fact, in daily childrearing of preschool children, parents should look for these kinds of social distinctions and tell the little boy he "looks just like daddy" when his clothes resemble dad's. The little girl will benefit when she's given her play cosmetics "just like mommy's." These things help to reinforce the crucial identification process which solidifies male identity in boys and female identity in girls.

These distinctions are important in childrearing. That is why the unisex myth which calls for "an end to all distinctions based on sex" is so destructive for normal sexual identification. Our culture has developed these sex-role stereotypes because they are useful in childrearing and they help reinforce adult sexual identities as well.

Culturally-defined, with Arbitrary But
Harmful Assignment

These sex-role stereotypes (see boxes 9 and 10) are arbitrary because, once again, there is no biological or moral basis for them. But unlike the category we just considered, these stereotypes are harmful and should be abolished in our society.

This category includes the harmful attitudes of male chauvinism that I described in chapter 1. It also includes the so-called masculine image of the menacing macho myth described in chapter 1.

This category further includes those arbitrary classifications of employment categories which hinder the individual's freedom to develop talents and abilities. If your little children want to play a game of "hospital," it would be morally wrong to insist that the girl *always* play the role of "nurse," letting only a little boy play the "doctor" role. These are the kind of arbitrary, harmful stereotypes that overrule the consideration of individual ability. Intelligence, not sex, should be a criterion for choosing a career as a physician, dentist, psychologist, or optometrist.

Destructive male stereotypes, such as telling lewd jokes, using crass locker-room language, and sexually harassing women are part of this category of harmful stereotypes.

Obviously, these are the types of sex-role stereotypes that concerned parents should not teach their children by either word or example. In fact, children need to be taught that these harmful stereotypes are morally wrong, when the children become aware of them in everyday life.

The existence of this category of harmful sex-role stereotypes provides fuel for the unisex proponents. But while this one category of sex-role distinctions needs to be eliminated in our society, it does not logically follow that the other four helpful types of sex-role distinctions need to be obliterated as well. Herein lies the fallacy of the unisex myth.

Special Help for Special Cases

If parents follow the guidelines I have just summarized, their children are unlikely to suffer any sexual-identity problems. But if a child does develop sexual-identity conflict, psychological intervention can help put the child back on the track of normal sexual identification.

In the footnotes, I have listed the references to the detailed procedures I have developed. These procedures are explained in professional journals and psychological and psychiatric textbooks. While a concerned parent can do many things to correct an emerging sexual-identity problem in his or her own child, there are occasions when the child's sexual-identity problem is so severe that consultation with a Christian counselor or a Christian clinical child psychologist or child psychiatrist is advisable.

However, many professionals are not yet aware of the specialized techniques that my research program has developed, because these techniques have been developed only over the past twelve years, and have been reported in the professional literature primarily in the past six years. This means that when many child psychotherapists were in school, they did not receive training in how to treat the problem, and if they have not researched the recent professional literature, they probably have not yet read the reports on this problem. Therefore, if the parent needs to consult a Christian counselor or a professional child psychotherapist, it would be advisable to provide the therapist with this book and request that the therapist look up the technical articles reporting on the treatment techniques.

The purpose of this book has not been to report on the specialized techniques that I have developed to treat children with sexual-identity problems. Instead this book has been addressed primarily to parents, teen-agers, and counselors who want to become more aware, in general, of the importance of monitoring childrens' sexual-identity development in order to detect the problem or in order to prevent the problem from really developing at all.

For this reason, I will not describe in much detail the variety of techniques that I have developed to deal with different aspects of sexual-identity problems in children. I will provide only an overview here and leave it to the reader to look up the technical articles if more detail is needed.

Treatment Techniques in the Clinic

In describing the treatments of Craig and Becky in chapters 8 and 9, I explained some of the ways either to train a child to have more appropriate sex-typed play or to train a parent to teach his or her own child to have normal play habits. In addition, I have developed other procedures to eliminate the feminine-sounding voice that many boys with sexual-identity problems have.

I have also developed comprehensive treatment procedures for boys who have extremely pronounced effeminate mannerisms and gestures which are difficult for parents to treat at home. Some of these procedures require a clinical psychologist who has access to a videotape machine for videotape feedback, in combination with some complex behavior-therapy training procedures. These procedures are designed to help the child discriminate more carefully what the feminine gestures are and then to train him to suppress those mannerisms one at a time.

Treatment Procedures in the Home

I have found that it is generally preferable to be able to involve the parents in the treatment programs for the children, as I did with Craig and his parents. However, I developed a variety of techniques which can be individually tailored to the child's problems and the home situation. That means that the token system I developed for Craig is just one example of some of the things that could be done at home. Older children, for example, respond better to a point-economy system rather than a token-economy system. Yet other children respond to other techniques to be used in the home, depending on what the child's particular problem is.

Some boys with sexual-identity problems need extensive training in athletic and masculine behaviors as the primary focus of their therapy, while other boys require both that masculine kind of training and training in suppressing or eliminating feminine behaviors. I found that it is important to keep careful behavioral records (like those I described for Craig) so that the child's progress can be carefully monitored to see whether the procedure at home is working.

Other Treatment Strategies

In some cases, it is necessary to introduce treatment procedures for the child in school. At this point, treatment usually requires the cooperation of a child psychologist who can carefully work with the teacher and principal to eliminate problems in the classroom, due to the child's sexual-identity problems and inappropriate sex-type behaviors. I have worked out programs in school to increase masculine game participation and to suppress feminine body gestures and speech patterns in boys.

I have also developed some athletic-behavior training procedures. For example, if the children at school often play softball and have skills in hitting a playground ball, then that would be one of the necessary skills to teach the sexual-identity disturbed boy in a non-threatening training procedure. It is always preferable to have the father involved in this training, and for the father to abstain from being critical of the boy's athletic performance. If there's not a father, a father substitute can be used.

What I do is work with one athletic skill at a time, starting out with easy tasks and gradually building up to greater proficiency. For example, the child may be asked to throw a ball short distances and gradually work up to longer and longer distances. This intensive practice is designed to be rewarding, without any criticism.

Sometimes it is necessary for the boy to have individual counseling or psychotherapy sessions to solve emotional problems and to develop a normal sexual identity. This is particularly true in children older than eight years. This usually is in conjunction with the other treatment procedures that I am describing.

For boys who lack a stable relationship with a father or father figure, I often try to build a "buddy" relationship between the boy and a "big brother." I find a male college student or other suitable "big brother" who can take the boy on outings, provide a healthy masculine model, and develop a relationship that gives the boy an opportunity to be with and feel emotionally close to a caring man.

Finally, I have also developed various approaches of "self-control" for the children. Examples of this include using the wrist counter, as I did with Becky, as well as other kinds of self-rewarding activities. These are somewhat complicated treatment strategies which again require the supervision of a trained child psychotherapist who has read my research reports.

Long-term Follow-up

Approximately once a year, I have asked independent psychologists to evaluate the children I treated. This evaluation is to determine whether the improvements in the children's sexual identities have remained over time, and to determine whether the children might need additional treatment. This long-term study has been conducted to find out whether these children will grow up to have normal heterosexual family life. So far, the results are very encouraging.

The Image: Male and Female

It is interesting that the unisex mentality is based upon the godless world view of relativistic humanism, which includes the radical feminist movement.[5] Those who call for "an end to all distinctions based on sex" are those who simultaneously endorse the "right" to abortion, homosexuality, and divorce. The unisex mentality, therefore, is an assault against sex.

The unisex mentality denies the existence of unique mother and father roles.

The unisex·mentality denies the existence of human rights for unborn babies.

5. See Braun and Rekers, *The Christian in an Age of Sexual Eclipse*, chapter 2, "The Rhetoric of Revolt: The Sexual Propaganda of Humanism," and chapter 3, "Drawing the Battle Lines: The Radical Challenge of Sexual Extremists."

The unisex mentality denies existence of the norm of heterosexuality by affirming the life-denying practice of homosexual acts.

The unisex mentality denies the existence of divine sanction for marital permanence by its approval of divorce.

In this sense, the unisex mentality denies the existence of God Himself, because it opposes the Judeo-Christian Scriptures' teaching about sexuality and family responsibility.

The Bible asserts: "So God created man in his own image, in the image of God he created him; male and female he created them" (Gen. 1:27). This means that sexuality in men and women reflects the "image of God." When the unisex mentality denies the human "distinctions based on sex," it is denying the *image of God* in the human personality. But what else would we expect from the *godless* world view of relativistic humanism? The unisex mentality denies the existence of God and His Word's authority, and in the same sweep, denies the mark of God in the human personality—the distinctions of male and female.

Fortunately, most parents sincerely want to shape normal sexual identities in their sons and daughters. They have two basic ways of accomplishing this: by assuming distinctive and proper roles of mothering and fathering their children, and by directly encouraging masculinity in their sons and femininity in their daughters.

Train a child in the way he should go, and when he is old he will not turn from it. [Prov. 22:6]

Index